HIDDEN HISTORY

of

ASHLAND,
OREGON

Merry Christmas! 2023

HIDDEN HISTORY
of
ASHLAND, OREGON

Joe Peterson

THE
History
PRESS

Published by The History Press
Charleston, SC
www.historypress.com

First published 2020

Manufactured in the United States

ISBN 9781467144919

Library of Congress Control Number: 2020932000

Notice: The information in this book is true and complete to the best of our knowledge. It is offered without guarantee on the part of the author or The History Press. The author and The History Press disclaim all liability in connection with the use of this book.

CONTENTS

CONTENTS

Acknowledgements

A shland has been blessed with a boatload of talented local historians. Both Kay Atwood and Marjorie O'Harra's works are featured in this historical narrative. Jeff LaLande, George Kramer, John Enders and Terry Skibby, with his vast collection of Ashland images, have all extensively chronicled the town's history. Their perspectives have been especially helpful when writing this book. Additionally, many researchers have contributed to this volume in varying degrees, and the citations of their specific works can be found in the bibliography.

Additional credit should be given to several individuals who contributed their thoughts as this book evolved, including Al Willstatter, Mike Dawkins, Betty LaDuke, Tim Rutter, Southern Oregon University campus officer Todd Doriguzzi, Larry Mullaly, Tom Kennedy, Holly Nowak, Mike Morris, Judie Bunch, Patrick Oropallo, Shirley Patton, Margaret Rubin, Vicki Bryden, Kira Lesley, Tessa Reed and David Biondi.

The stockpiles of information regarding Ashland history that are referenced in this book include the Oregon Shakespeare Festival (OSF) Archives, Southern Oregon Historical Society's (SOHS) research library, the Ashland Public Library and Southern Oregon University's (SOU) Hannon Library. The exceedingly helpful staff members at the SOHS Research Library, OSF Archives and the Lithia Auto Group consistently answered my research questions and provided me access to their image collection.

Special thanks go to my editors, Laurie Krill and Ashley Hill and The History Press's production crew, who guided me through the production phase, and Stephanie Peterson, who provided initial proofreading.

INTRODUCTION

The study of the past is a constantly evolving, never-ending journey of discovery.
—historian Eric Foner

There is nothing about which everything has been done and said.
—Ida Tarbell

Ever since writing *Ashland*, an overview of the town's history for Arcadia Publishing, I have wanted to uncover the lesser-known stories of Ashland, Oregon, and provide a different look at the ones I had previously written. This book includes twenty-five vignettes from Ashland's past, and I hope my approach to these stories leaves readers with a new look at what is familiar and some surprises regarding what was previously unknown. I have not written about many of the topics in this book in the past, yet some are renditions, with different emphases and focuses.

I had not previously written about Ashland murders, famous best-selling authors Vladimir Nabokov and Johnny Gruelle or any of the homegrown innovators who are featured in Part III. From time to time, I had heard mention of some of these individuals and their entrepreneurial skills, but I simply hadn't pursued their stories until now. Political topics have always drawn my interest, so I included a chapter (in Part IV) on some political stories that I have framed in a somewhat different light. These tales include those of Rutherford Hayes, Theodore Roosevelt, Andrew Carnegie and John Kennedy.

Part V of this book is full of questions about why certain events happened in Ashland. For example, any discussion or photograph of the Ku Klux Klan in Ashland begs the question of how the group could have ever been active in what many today believe is, politically, a liberally leaning town. Also included in this section of the book is a condensed version of the story about the odd arrival of the Liberty Bell that I wrote for a Southern Oregon Historical Society newsletter a while back. It still seems to be a little-known historical event. Further, I have been intrigued why Erskine Caldwell's ashes reside in an Ashland cemetery when he never lived in the town.

For years, I have played golf on Ashland's 1927 course, which has a small cemetery just off the fourth green. I never really knew why the cemetery was there, but after considerable research, I found the answer, and I included it in this book. Thanks to the luck of finding an 1884 photograph of Ashland's town baseball team, I was able to enjoy tracking down the stories of their exploits, and I gained an insight into how different early baseball was.

Today, Ashland's award-winning Shakespeare Festival draws visitors to town, and it, along with Chautauqua, is addressed in Part VII. But what were the festival's predecessors? It appears that Ashland has always reinvented itself. I had no idea, for example, that a "hands-on healer" was a larger economic draw than Shakespeare for nearly two decades! Likewise, I didn't realize that touring motorists went to the city-operated Lithia Park campgrounds in such huge numbers that they were vital to the local economy for numerous years.

Vandalism has been an ongoing threat to Ashland's historical monuments for a very long time. Ashland hasn't had to deal with the same controversies that other American cities have had to face over their statues, but it can't seem to keep them intact either. Ashland also faces the contemporary danger of forest fires, which makes this book's story about Ashland's 1959 fire and the threat it posed to the town worth reading about. Part VIII of this book also includes a piece on urban legends and how important it is to question often-repeated stories and assumptions about the past. Finally, major historical events, such as the Holocaust, are difficult, at best, to comprehend without a personal connection. Longtime Ashland civic activist Al Willstatter's story, which is included in this book, may help in this regard.

PART I
MURDER *THEY* WROTE

I

A Very Cold Case

The murder of town doctor David Sisson has remained unsolved for 160 years. Yet a main street and an elementary school in Ashland are currently named after a possible suspect.

D r. David Sisson and his wife, Celeste Sisson, must have been rather exotic-looking as they dismounted from a well-equipped pack train near a clearing with few residents and a handful of structures. Here was an English-born physician accompanied by his wife, the daughter of French immigrants, who was young and attractive, even when covered in dust, and likely half his age. The couple's valuable pack animals and impressive equipment likely did not go unnoticed either.

Dr. Sisson and Celeste had just come from a long stretch in California and seemed interested in a break, even if it was in the sparse settlement that had recently been named Ashland Mills. A flour mill, boardinghouse, blacksmith shop, outbuildings and a small river (or creek) were all visible to the Sissons as they stood in the middle of what is today Ashland's downtown plaza. From this spot, if they peered far enough downstream, they could also spot what appeared to be a sawmill and two frame houses.

Wasting no time in improving the frontier settlement that he helped name and held the pending land title to much of, Abel Helman greeted the new stranger in town and encouraged him to stay permanently. Helman told him that the village had no doctor and that one could not be found for miles around; he also pointed out that Dr. Sisson could make a good living if he stayed. Helman must have been persuasive, because, within days of his respite from the trail, David Sisson offered to buy the only thing in the town that resembled a hotel, the Ashland Boardinghouse, where he and Celeste had been staying.

But there was a problem; the boardinghouse's previous owner, Morris Howell, didn't exactly have a deed. He had purchased the property from Abel Helman, who had previously taken out a donation land claim but had not received a government land patent yet. But there was no need to worry. Helman agreed, in writing, to give Howell a deed as soon as he could. Helman offered Sisson the same deal, and he took it, offering his pack animals and equipment as partial payment to Howell. Not content to simply run the boardinghouse, Sisson practiced medicine on the property as well. He eventually built a small wood structure nearby, which served as a hospital. Meanwhile, Celeste cooked meals and cleaned rooms for the mostly single men who stayed at the boardinghouse. David and Celeste even ran a small dry goods store at the boardinghouse, and they seemed, through all of these endeavors, to have won a degree of the village's respect and increase in their net worth. Eventually, the Sissons were doing well enough financially to buy 160 acres just outside of town, where they planned to build a house and a farm.

However, on March 11, 1858, a man lay in wait to shoot David Sisson. The man succeeded in wounding him, as the shotgun sprayed the doctor's hands and side with buckshot. A report from the *Oregon Sentinel*, Southern Oregon's source for news, said that the man's name was Beckett and that he had fled the area. Ten days after the assassination attempt, the Sisson barn was burned, destroying the structure and killing their animals. Just five days after this chaos, Celeste gave birth to Augusta Rebecca Sisson.

Augusta would never know her father, as Dr. David Sisson was gunned down in a second assassination attempt just seven days after her birth— he could not be saved. The single ball shot came from a high tree, not far from the creek and Abel Helman's house. Three local men heard the shot, but they were not able to identify the culprit; they carried Sisson's body to Celeste. A jury inquest was quickly assembled at the doctor's hospital building, and each man gave his account. Perhaps coincidently, the justice of the peace for the community of Ashland Mills, Abel Helman, resigned the same day. Helman's resignation was followed the next day by the resignation of Constable George Good. Meanwhile, Dr. David Sisson's body was buried without any examination—case closed. However, the prosecuting attorney for Jackson County was appalled to hear that no attempt had been made to

Dr. David Sisson's gravestone. His murder remains unsolved. *Author's collection.*

remove the fatal ball that felled David Sisson. An urgent letter was sent to the county coroner, urging him to dig up the three-day-old gravesite and extract the lead bullet from the corpse. The graveside inquest, of sorts, resulted in no identified killer. Referring to the murder as "cold-blooded" and "cowardly," a Jacksonville newspaper pleaded for someone to come forward with a name, but no one did.

Celeste Sisson was now a widow with a very young child. Assuming her worst troubles were over, Celeste retreated to her farmhouse outside of town, where she was, once again, a victim. Just a few months after the loss of her husband, Celeste's house was set on fire in her absence. She must have wondered if the assassin had come back—or if they had ever really left. A month after the arson, Sisson's estate was in probate court, with her appointed lawyer selling its dwindling assets to pay debts. The farmhouse, along with its contents and the barn, had been burned; the hospital had been sold; and the boardinghouse had been rented, leaving Celeste with a small sum of money and a city lot. But she was, essentially, homeless.

A year later, the rented boardinghouse was also set on fire. Along with the total loss of the building, the town's post office and the existing legal records and maps for Ashland Mills, which were both located within the boardinghouse, were lost. Town gossip blamed a transient for the blaze. Hanes True, who had worked, on and off, for the Sisson's at the boardinghouse before the murder of Dr. Sisson, married Celeste two years later. With her new marriage and a daughter to raise, Celeste labored on, living in the new farmhouse that Hanes had built for her. It seemed as if the Sisson's case had finally closed.

David Sisson's will left his remaining property to both his wife and his infant daughter. Upon reaching legal age, Augusta Sisson asked her mother more questions about her father. Celeste told her about the shooting, the fires and her entitlement to a part of her father's property—the case was reopened. At the age of twenty-one, Augusta hired an attorney and surveyor and sued several pioneer pillars of the community, including Abel Helman and Eber Emery, both early Ashland Mills businessmen. What ensued was a two-year-long court battle, retracing everything, from Dr. Sisson's murder to the destroyed legal records and maps. Augusta wanted what she said was hers. Her attorney claimed that Helman had defrauded her father and mother and had, for years, been selling the land that was rightfully theirs. The defendant's rebuttal denied fraud and, more importantly, any suggestion that A.D. Helman was in any way behind the fires that consumed the Sisson properties. Twenty-four years after her father's murder, Augusta lost the lawsuit to recover his property, and she additionally had to pay the defendants' court costs. In 1882, the case was once again closed.

Historian A.G. Walling, in his 1884 history of southern Oregon, once again addressed the murder, if only as a passing, shameful mention. Walling described it as well-planned and executed, but that was all that his investigation revealed. According to Walling, theories were still plentiful a full twenty-six years after the murder, but no one was ever caught, and no cause was ever discovered. However, when the town of Ashland reached the one hundredth anniversary of its founding in 1952, a centennial party was held. Fittingly, the *Ashland Daily Tidings* released a one-hundred-year history of the town, including an article titled, "First Murder Still Mystery." At this late date, the case was ninety-four years old, but it was obviously still of interest and note—not to the town's police department and courts, of course, as too much time had passed. The remaining cold trail of the case was full of conflicting and piecemeal evidence, which meant the investigation was left for an interested historian to untangle.

Likely intrigued because the cold case had so much to do with the founding of her chosen town, Kay Atwood, the author of several southern Oregon histories, took up the challenge of solving Dr. Sisson's murder in her 1987 book, *Mill Creek Journal*. While she was in the process of researching the early years of Ashland Mills, between 1850 and 1860, Atwood discovered a most intriguing letter that had been tucked away for 125 years in the papers of pioneer E.K. Anderson. Written in 1858, the account claimed to be that of an eye witness to the Sisson murder. Nearly 130 years after the murder, had Atwood found the smoking gun? Had the case been reopened?

In the letter, S.B. Olmstead claimed that he recognized and saw the killer up close but did not dare name him. Olmstead alluded to a matching bullet and gun, a distinct boot track, a hostile attitude toward the doctor and a friendship with Beckett, who was thought to have been Sisson's previous assassin. Still, Olmstead said he would not testify against such a well-

Kay Atwood's classic study of early Ashland. *Courtesy of Southern Oregon Historical Society.*

known man. Atwood's extensive research pointed toward a powerful and influential town founder, public official and developer of numerous businesses: Abel Helman. He seemed to be in constant debt and needed money to pay the court judgments against him. Atwood's research also led her to the conclusion that David Sisson and his wife had become some the wealthiest settlers and landowners in Ashland Mills just two years after they became residents. Nevertheless, after the most extensive investigation of the murder to date, Atwood could still not directly name Helman as the man who fired the fatal shot, and the case was closed.

In 2017, a television report by the channel KDRV reopened the case and concluded that the likely culprit was the person who had the most to gain, financially, from the murder: Abel Helman. The report further disclosed a curious "new" addition to the Ashland Mountain View Cemetery, which had been established in the early 1900s; Dr. David Sisson's 1858 gravestone. It seems that the cemetery office received a phone call from property owners in the Emigrant Lake Reservoir area indicating that they had an old tombstone and wanted the city's cemetery sexton to come and get it. Not knowing what to do with a gravestone that far predated the cemetery, the sexton did some serious research. Interestingly enough, the records they found showed that Celeste had been buried with her second husband, Haynes, in the Ashland Mountain View Cemetery in 1909. The decision was made to place Dr. Sisson's stone next to their grave marker, reuniting David and Celeste. The case of Dr. Sisson's mysterious murder is closed—for now.

2

OFFICERS DOWN

The memorial stone is difficult to locate; you have to know where to look. It's not near the site of the killing, although it used to be. The granite monument had been located, for over seventy years, on the island divider near the corner of Siskiyou Boulevard and Union Street. Today, it can be found at 1155 East Main Street, between two flag poles. It reads: "In Memory of Sam Prescott—Victor Knott, killed in the line of duty, 1931." Originally placed at the spot of young Ashland police officer Sam Prescott's murder, the monument has since been moved to the city police station, about a half-mile to the northeast.

In a 1962 newspaper article, Ashland historian and journalist Marjorie O'Harra found the murder of the two police officers hard to comprehend. As a lifelong Ashlander, she knew how abnormal this event was. Since the release of Marjorie's feature article, nearly sixty years ago, several other writers have also found the story both tragic and seemingly out of character for the small town of Ashland. The execution of Officer Prescott's killer had barely occurred when merchant policeman Victor Knott was gunned down at the corner of Pioneer and A Streets.

It was 7:00 a.m. on a cold Saturday in January, when traffic officer Prescott noticed a suspicious-looking car traveling south on Siskiyou Boulevard. The De Soto automobile wasn't speeding, but its left-rear window was broken out. Prescott was always on the prowl for possible bootleggers and car thieves, so he followed the car. Prescott was something of a hometown hero; born and raised in Ashland, the twenty-five-year-old officer had developed quite

Above: The 1931 fallen officer's memorial stone was once located where Officer Sam Prescott was gunned down. *Courtesy of the Ashland Police Department.*

Left: Twenty-five-year-old Ashland police officer Sam Prescott. *Courtesy of the Ashland Police Department.*

a reputation in his three and a half years on the job. In fact, just a couple of days before his fatal traffic stop, Prescott had seized over thirty cases of illegal alcohol and arrested the rumrunner.

Several aspects of the Prescott case seem unique, including an eyewitness account from a twelve-year-old, a hitchhiker's testimony, an extremely lengthy confession from the killer, wild rumors of a "professional hit," talk of lynching parties and the swiftness of the trial. Even the fact that no one moved Prescott's body from where it lay face down on the road, for nearly a half hour after he was killed seems insensitive, at best.

"The way he fell, it made me and my mamma sick—he laid so still," sobbed fifth-grader Allen Batchelor. He and his mother happened to be walking along Siskiyou Boulevard, on their way to visit a neighbor, when the shots were fired, and they saw Prescott fall. But the horrified pair were not the only eyewitnesses to the murder. The driver of the suspicious out-of-state car, James Kingsley, had previously picked up a hitchhiker in Cottage Grove who occupied the front passenger seat throughout the entire ordeal. Eighteen-year-old Earl Remington gave the other riveting eyewitness account. Held as a material witness, Remington explained that when Prescott questioned Kingsley during the traffic stop, Kingsley admitted that he did not have either a car registration or a driver's license. When Prescott tried to commandeer the car, Kingsley shot him a total of three times as Remington clutched the passenger door in both confusion and fear. Kingsley then sped south out of town, leaving his passenger no time to escape. Fearing for his own life, Remington took the first chance he had to escape and ran when Kingsley decided to ditch the car on a dirt road just south of Ashland. Remington ran to an old farmhouse and told the owner call the Ashland Police Station. Within an hour and a half, Kingsley was in custody.

On seven typed pages, James Kingsley admitted to everything, including numerous robberies, car thefts and previous jail time. His confession culminated with the shooting of Officer Prescott. He even detailed his life story, which included orphanages, reform schools, holdups and car thefts in several states. His concluding paragraph read, "If the state wants to hang me, that is all right, but I could do no good dead. If I am permitted to live and receive life imprisonment, I would be able to do some good by being a living example that crime doesn't pay."

As the trial went on, rumors circulated that Kingsley was part of an organized plot and had been sent by southern Oregon rumrunners to get rid of a nemesis. Even the district attorney implied that Kingsley may have been connected to some kind of plot. A report spread that said Kingsley had stopped north of Ashland and inquired if Prescott was still on duty that morning. Maybe he had been given a physical description of Prescott. Earl Remington, the hitchhiker, said that he also thought Kingsley was possibly connected with big-time criminals. In his confession, however, Kingsley denied ever knowing, or knowing of, Prescott. In addition to these rumors, for several days, there were threats of a lynch mob forming in Ashland, which resulted in the transfer of Kingsley to Medford, where he was placed in the same secure cell that held the notorious DeAutremont brothers three years earlier. "There is an angry rumbling as the crowd pressing around the police station seeks a glimpse of James Kingsley," reported the *Ashland Daily Tidings.*

With a complete confession in hand, a grand jury indicted Kingsley on the charge of first-degree murder within nine days of Prescott's death. The jury really only had to decide whether his sentence would be life in prison or death by hanging. Kingsley's court-appointed lawyers argued that things happened so fast on the morning of the shooting that Kingsley basically didn't know what he was doing. The prosecution, however, argued premeditation, based on Kingsley's final shot into the officer's back, which he took while Prescott was already lying in the road. Kingsley's defense and argument for life in prison boiled down to the argument that he was a victim of his devastating childhood and that he had previously been a model prisoner. His lawyers also argued that the three DeAutremont brothers, the cold-blooded killers who murdered four innocent Southern Pacific train men, had received life sentences rather than the death penalty. But a mere eleven days after the murder of Prescott, the jury, which did not include anyone from Ashland, reached a speedy two-hour unanimous verdict that the defendant was to be hanged. Despite numerous appeals, including one to the state supreme court and the governor, Kingsley was executed at the Oregon state prison in Salem, just nine months after taking Officer Prescott's life.

Twenty-six days, less than a month, after the execution of Kingsley, yet another Ashland police officer was murdered on November 19, 1931. This time, the murder took place in the railroad district, at the site of a large warehouse on the corner of Pioneer and A Streets. Officers Victor Knott and Roy Layman were on a night patrol in the city police car, when they approached the warehouse and spotted two men in the shadow of the building. It was 11:00 p.m., so Knott rolled down the driver's-side window of the Chevrolet sedan and yelled out at them, asking what they were doing there. Likely assuming that the officers knew that they had broken into the building, the men began firing their pistols directly at the officers, killing Knott instantly with three shots. Layman bolted from the car and shot several return rounds, which were greeted by even more gun fire as the men escaped. Officer Layman was unhurt, but nothing could be done to save his partner.

Layman's call for help resulted in roadblocks in all directions and a frantic search for the killers. A search party of armed Ashland men was quickly assembled and led by the local sheriff. At 3:00 a.m., a call came in from the state police, who reported that, near the town of Gold Hill, a speeding Wills-Knight sedan had

Ashland police officer Victor Knott was shot and killed in 1931. *Courtesy of the Ashland Police Department.*

careened over an embankment while it was being pursued by a state police officer. Just before the crash, two men were seen leaping from the car and running into the surrounding hills. Upon a further examination of the car's contents, the state police found a colt revolver and army discharge papers on the front seat.

The next morning, a huge posse of nearly two hundred armed private citizens attempted to search for the men in the rugged hillsides; they used bloodhounds and even an airplane, but they were unsuccessful. A few days later, two men were seen running from an old cabin in the Green Springs area, and the search was shifted to the east of Ashland. Meanwhile the pistol, car and army papers were traced back to Denver, Colorado, and the name Albert W. Reed. What's more, the shots that killed Knott were found to be from the gun that had been found in the car.

Denver police eventually caught up to Reed, who had made his way back to Colorado, and on January 4, 1932, they sent him to Jackson County, Oregon, to face a trial on the charge of first-degree murder. Reed's partner in crime was never found. At the March 1 trial, Officer Layman positively identified Reed as the man who fired the shots that killed his partner. It only took the jury twenty hours to find Reed guilty, but they found him guilty of second-degree murder, not first-degree murder. Reed was sentenced three days later to life in prison, but he only served a little more than ten years before he was given a commutation of his sentence by Oregon governor Sprague in December 1942.

A trip to either murder site today will turn up no monuments or memorials. The intersection of Siskiyou Boulevard and Union Street remains a non-disrupt, grassy island divider, and the railroad district warehouse has served a number of purposes without any reference to a sad shootout. Perhaps it's for the best; murder sites don't always make the best memorials, and these 1931 events have thankfully been, what town historian Marjorie O'Harra called, tragic aberrations.

PART II
BEST SELLERS

3

LOLITA, BUTTERFLIES AND RAGGEDY ANN AND ANDY

It is difficult to imagine two more disparate authors than Vladimir Nabokov and Johnny Gruelle, yet both spent some of their most creative time in Ashland, Oregon, finishing their incredibly different best-selling works.

LOLITA AND BUTTERFLIES

A rather large rattlesnake, a vagabond son and a never-before-visited alpine setting seemed to be what brought Vladimir and Vera Nabokov to Ashland in the first days of June 1953. Russian-born Professor Nabokov spent his summers pursuing his hobby of collecting butterflies in the mountainous areas of the American West. He and his wife, Vera, traveled every year, putting thousands of miles on their worn Oldsmobile. In the summer of 1953, the pair planned to travel to Arizona and, later, the Pacific Northwest, specifically Oregon. However, Arizona's weather turned unseasonably cool and windy—not great for butterfly hunting. Additionally, Vera was terrified after she watched her husband kill a large rattlesnake near their door one morning. At that point, both of them were ready to move on. Their next stop was Ashland, Oregon, where they arranged to rent a small house for the summer months. The pair also saw their move to the north as an opportunity to be closer to their son, Dmitri, who had been working on a road construction project in Oregon.

Never doubting that southern Oregon and California's northern coast would be wonderful butterfly hunting country, Vladimir and Vera moved into the home of Professor Arthur Taylor, who was traveling in the east for the summer. Taylor, at the time, was the popular head of the Department of Social Sciences at Southern Oregon College of Education (now Southern Oregon University). Today, a hall on the Ashland campus bears his name. Nabokov apparently enjoyed the setting at 163 Meade Street, which he called the "Ashland Headquarters." The house was small but boasted a garden ringed in flowers, and it was situated high on the hill, away from the main boulevard.

Once Nabokov settled into his disciplined, self-described, daily workday, he would spend his mornings in Ashland, roaming the nearby hills in search of butterflies, until noon. After lunch, he would concentrate on completing his erotic novel, *Lolita*, until dinnertime. Only on cloudy days, which were not conducive to netting new butterflies, would Nabokov change his daily schedule. His compositional approach to writing consisted of him first putting his thoughts on index cards and later transcribing them, in longhand, into chapters. Vera would then type the manuscript, and they would both proofread.

Nabokov praised his time in Ashland as particularly fruitful, for both butterfly collecting and writing. It was not uncommon for him to hike more than fifteen miles a day to locate rare butterflies. *Lolita*, too, came right along after he made several visits to the local college library for research. Vera described the area as having lush, green hills, and overall, it had been a very satisfying place.

In the fall, after Nabokov had returned to his professorship at Cornell University, he had the task of trying to get his wildly controversial novel into print. It was, he insisted, the best thing he had ever written, yet he knew it could cost him his job. What developed was a two-pronged problem, for he was sure he would lose his job if he did not print *Lolita* anonymously. Further, all of the major American publishing houses had initially turned the book down, as they felt it was far too pornographic and likely to be banned. In addition to this, the owners of the publishing houses feared prosecution.

In 1955, the only copies of *Lolita* to surface were those of a French edition that had been printed in English, and they clearly identified Nabokov as the author. Nabokov had been convinced by others that there was no way to keep his identity a secret once the book was published. Often smuggled into the United States, *Lolita*, ironically and rapidly made Nabokov the most popular instructor on Cornell's campus. His classes filled quickly, and students sought his autograph. With the 1958 publication of *Lolita* in the

Left: The wildly successful novel that was finished in Ashland, where author Nabokov also hunted butterflies. *Author's collection.*

Right: A plaque acknowledging the site where one of the world's top ten novels was completed in 1953. *Photograph courtesy of Terry Skibby.*

United States, sales soared; one hundred thousand hardcover books were sold in just three weeks. At that point, Vladimir was rich and able to resign his professorship to concentrate solely on his writings. Nabokov was even offered the chance to make a Hollywood movie of *Lolita*. To date, more than sixty million copies of the book have been sold worldwide.

Unfortunately, the small cottage where the Nabokovs spent their Ashland summer of 1953 burned in September 1999. *Lolita* fans on a pilgrimage will now find two modern townhouses and a commemorative plaque on the site where the Taylor house once stood. The plaque reads: "On this site, in 1953, Russian writer Vladimir Nabokov (1899–1977) completed his notorious novel *Lolita*."

RAGGEDY ANN AND ANDY

By the time author and illustrator Johnny Gruelle had steered his special-order six-cylinder bus up Granite Street, he and his family had been on the road for four months. When he arrived in Ashland, on the afternoon of August 28, 1923, Gruelle parked the most unusual-looking motor coach in

The Gruelle family arrives in Ashland to live on Granite Street in 1923. *Photograph courtesy of Terry Skibby.*

front of 108 Granite Street. Gruelle's longtime friend and fellow spiritualist Emma Oeder had urged him to come out west to Ashland, as she had. Emma, along with her husband and daughter, had met the Gruelle family a dozen years earlier in Connecticut, where they became fast friends and often held séances together.

Gruelle, exhausted from his nonstop pursuit of freelance cartooning and illustration work, was always looking for a gentrified adventure and had been receiving glowing letters from Emma about the town of Ashland for months. She wrote of the town's rivers, teeming with fish; the moderate climate; Chautauqua's entertainment; Lithia's water fountains; the majestic mountains; and a kind of artist colony of creative folks, including Zane Grey, Bert Moses and Irving Vining, all awaited his arrival. Emma, a psychic enthusiast, also offered Johnny and Myrtle Gruelle the promise of evening séances. The likely clincher for the Gruelles, though, was Emma's offer of the use of her guest house for as long as they wanted it. Johnny could not resist such a cross-country lark, even if it required a lot of advance planning. The trip needed to be a working-vacation, providing a steady income. Gruelle would also need to somehow both drive the bus and find time to do his artistic work along the way. Ever mindful of his need for income, Johnny arranged to have his commission checks sent to towns along the route to southern Oregon.

The Gruelles' bus was no ordinary rig. It was painted tan and brown and had been completely redone on the inside, with leather seats that became bunks at night, curtains, storage areas and a radio. Such a traveling home would have attracted attention in any motor camp, even without Gruelle's paintings of Raggedy Ann and Andy on its sides. The Gruelles' trip out to Oregon was one long camping experience and included numerous stops along the way for picnics and sightseeing. Johnny set aside breaks every day so that he could continue to work on his comic strips and keep the checks coming.

When the Gruelles arrived, the addition of four more people and a dog quickly made Emma's house seem too small for everyone. So, the Gruelle family soon moved into the promised guest house on the corner of the Oeder property. Small, but with a terrific view of Lithia Park below, the rectangular house at 114 Granite became the family's home for one and a half years. Both Gruelle children were enrolled in Ashland schools, and Myrtle tended to domestic chores and participated in the very active local Women's Civic Improvement Club. Johnny quickly went to work on his many commissions

Johnny Gruelle loved to fish at nearby rivers and lakes when he was not writing Raggedy Ann stories. *Courtesy of Southern Oregon Historical Society.*

Try This

To feel cool without you must be cool within. Try this as a sure cure for heat-a-monia: Get a visual picture of the tastiest, the most enticing and the coolest thing you can think of—then put on your hat and go to the—

RAGGEDY ANN SWEET SHOP

Ask for your favorite and forget the heat. It's a sure and quick cure. Try it!

The Raggedy Ann
SWEET SHOP

An advertisement for the Raggedy Ann and Andy Sweet Shop, which was located in the Enders building in downtown Ashland. *Courtesy of the Terry Skibby collection.*

but always found time to take his boys fishing. Their evenings in Ashland often included séances with Emma and other friends, and weekend trips to Emma's very rustic Lake of the Woods cabin were also common.

In town, Johnny was easily recognized as the famous creator of Raggedy Ann and Andy, which meant he was regularly stopped by folks who wanted him to sign their dolls and books. One Main Street store displayed his work in its front window, and in the Enders building, a soda parlor displayed wall murals that were specially painted by Gruelle. Emma had also asked her close friend to do the paintings for her ice cream shop, which she named the Raggedy Ann Sweet Shoppe when Johnny came to town. Along with Johnny, novelist Zane Grey, national columnist Bert Moses and professor and town-booster Irving Vining formed a cadre of town intellectuals and friends.

Johnny's new friends, as well as Emma and daughter, Lynda, were invited to celebrate New Year's in 1924 at the recently completed Women's Civic Clubhouse, just down the hill from the Oeder property and across from Lithia Park. The Gruelles provided their guests with dinner and dancing, and Johnny entertained on the piano. The Gruelles often invited friends to parties at the clubhouse during their stay in Ashland.

By early 1924, Johnny had written a new Raggedy book, his first in four years. Titled *Raggedy Ann and Andy and the Camel with the Wrinkled Knees*, the book's elaborate illustrations were drawn at Emma's cabin at Lake of the

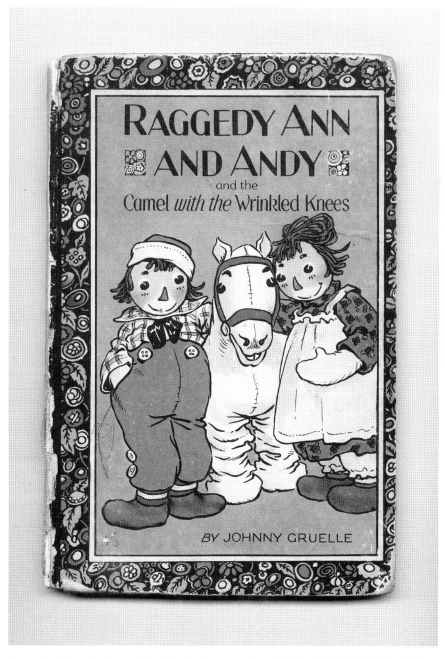

Best-selling Raggedy Ann and Andy book that was written in Ashland in 1924. *Author's collection.*

Woods, where he often worked. A toy camel that he had purchased for his boys was his inspiration. Metal rods, which had been designed to strengthen the camel's legs, poked through the fabric and seemed dangerous, so Johnny removed them, resulting in a toy camel with wrinkled fabric knees. This book became one of his best-selling and most beloved stories.

Near the end of 1924, this seemingly idyllic time in Ashland was disrupted when tragedy struck. Johnny's son Worth contracted scarlet fever and had to be taken to the town hospital. A few days later, Johnny joined Worth in the same hospital, as he was suffering from blockages in both his kidneys and bladder that left him near death at the age of forty-three. Nevertheless, within a few weeks, both had recovered. As a firm believer in psychic signs, Gruelle concluded that this was an omen. It was time for them to leave.

The Gruelles' possessions were given away, and their wonderful bus was sold, as Johnny was still too weak to drive across the country again. This time, the family took a train back to Connecticut. Patricia Hall later wrote what must be the best-researched and most complete biography of Gruelle, *Johnny Gruelle Creator of Raggedy Ann and Andy*. At one point, Hall speculated that had illness not interfered, Johnny and Myrtle might have stayed in Ashland permanently, as they enjoyed the slower pace of life that the small town had to offer. But this was not to be.

PART III
HOMEGROWN INNOVATORS

It never looks like history when you are living through it.
—John W. Gardner

4
SPOTTED OWLS, LINCOLN LOGS AND MOUSE TRAPS

Turning Trash into Cash on Helman Street

Mouse Traps and Lincoln Logs, Too?

Jim Parsons didn't enter his formative years determined to build a better mouse trap—that came later. After graduating from Ashland High School in 1936, Parsons attended Southern Oregon Normal School, where he met Angus Bowmer and decided to try his hand at acting. Bowmer was operating a fledgling Shakespeare festival in the summers of 1937 and 1938, when he cast Parsons as Sebastian in *Twelfth Night*, among several other roles. After graduating from the University of Oregon, Parsons served in the navy during World War II and, afterward, started an inter-island shipping business in the Philippines. This, unfortunately, led to Parsons contracting several tropical diseases, and he soon returned to Ashland to recover.

Parsons eventually started a career in radio and television broadcasting (his college major), which meant he often lived in big cities, without easy access to hunting and fishing. So, in 1949, he decided to build a box factory on Helman Street that would supply the orchards in the valley. At that time, timber was plentiful in the area, and scrap lumber from local mills was being burned as trash. "Trim ends were going straight to the burner. They weren't even going into chips," he once exclaimed in disgust. As a leader in recycling wood products for fifty years under the business name Parsons Pine Products, Jim Parsons believed in converting wood waste into profit and, accordingly, full-time jobs. "We even sold the sawdust to chicken farmers and dairies," he said.

Jim Parsons supplied mouse trap blanks made from recycled wood scraps worldwide. *Author's collection.*

When the orchards started using cardboard for their boxes, Parsons found that the Fisher Price and Mattel toy companies were eager to buy all of the small wooden pieces he could produce for their toy lines, including Lincoln Logs and dollhouse frames. Always on the lookout for new opportunities, Parsons also added mouse and rat trap wooden bases, louvre slats and door and window parts to the company's ever-expanding line of products. Parsons later identified an unmet demand for smooth wood blanks and rapidly became "the largest mouse trap blank manufacturer in the world," according to a case study that was done by Catherine M. Mater in the 1990s titled *Parsons Pine Products: Trash to Cash.* He built most of the company's machinery himself, including a sand belt cleaner, and he engineered extra smooth saw blades that left wood surfaces easier to print on without gumming up. Parsons's goal was always the same: use every inch of the raw product possible and provide a number of incentives for employees.

Parsons Pine Products prospered and grew from its original three-employee staff into a workforce of more than one hundred, filling the niche markets that few aside from Jim Parsons saw. His prescient ideas didn't stop with improved technology; he also included innovative incentives for his workforce, including well pay, safety pay, and profit-sharing, well before others implemented these motivational carrots. Both well pay and safety pay rewarded workers who were on the job every day, without injuries or mistakes, with either an extra day's pay or a day off. His philosophy was that "people should be paid for what they do, not what they don't do." Profit-sharing has since become a common practice in smaller businesses through various bonus plans. Parsons gained national attention when he paid his workers to not to get sick or have accidents, and all three concepts have since become commonplace in texts on management.

Employee training at Parsons Pine Products was ongoing and often illustrated with physical demonstrations. One example Parsons used involved him building a pyramid of mouse trap blanks and knocking off the top portion of the stack. "There goes $10,000 through carelessness!" he exclaimed. The company's diverse product line, including knife blocks, wine racks, CD boxes, shoe organizers, special drawers, door louvers, toy blocks, mouse trap bases and Lincoln Logs, all came from former "trash" forest products. At one point, Parsons was even negotiating a deal with Japanese fish cake manufacturers that sold their products on boards slightly longer than a mousetrap. Larger wood product companies were dependent on the boom-and-bust cycle of the housing market, while Parsons was able to ship his specialized wood pieces across the country and overseas free of such concerns.

Seemingly a believer in teachable moments, Parsons, in 1980, decided to make both his employees and the wider community of Ashland aware of just how important niche businesses like his were to the local economy by paying his one hundred employees with two-dollar bills. "We had the bank bring them in, and a year later, some bills were still circulating in town." It was an economic lesson that Parsons just couldn't resist. Much of the innovation going on at 255 Helman Street was largely unknown outside of those who were intrigued by the occasional news article about Parsons.

Lincoln Logs were some of the numerous products made by Parsons Pine Products. *Author's collection.*

Ironically, it was the listing of the spotted owl as an endangered species in 1990 and the resulting loss of thousands of jobs in the wood products industry that focused attention on the small woodworking plant in Ashland, Oregon. Severe cutbacks meant that the industry needed to think of a new way to survive. Parsons Pine Products had successfully bucked business trends for nearly fifty years by making use of inferior and short wood scraps, but with the exception of those who purchased their products, the nearby Shakespeare festival, where Parsons had once performed, was much better known than the company.

This economic downturn led to a series of case studies that focused on making more with less by adapting more value-added wood product manufacturing—the very thing that Jim Parsons had been doing all along. The study by Catherine M. Mater titled, *Parsons Pine Product: Trash to Cash*, was the result. Somewhat under the radar for years, Parsons's "trash" factory and business philosophy became part of a broad study, which consequently increased their interest. The business was eventually sold in 1997, after Parsons's retirement.

Currently, a large part of the Parsons Pine Products warehouse is occupied by Baxter Fitness Solutions, which specializes in exercise for adults over the age fifty. Andy Baxter is the company's founder and is a certified medical exercise and post rehab–conditioning specialist. Baxter, not unlike Parsons, has been an innovator in his field, developing numerous exercise machines and concepts of strength and conditioning since he opened his original Ashland gym in 1997.

5

GOING BALLISTIC IN ASHLAND, OREGON

It took John Nosler seven shots to bring down that bull-moose, and it was a clean shot!

A dmittedly, the British Columbia moose was covered in a thick coat of mud and mostly hidden by dense willows, requiring the Ashland truck company owner John Nosler to sneak up close to kill it. Nevertheless, he placed his initial shot exactly where it needed to go to bring the moose down, but the bullet failed to penetrate the vital organs and kill the animal quickly. Nosler was a true marksman, having won numerous competitive shooting awards, but the bullet had expanded excessively, and several additional shots were required. On a previous hunting trip, he encountered a somewhat different problem when a dead-on shot from several hundred yards away failed to expand, leaving too narrow a wound. Nosler had to track the bull for hours after his first solid shot. So, in the fall of 1946, he was a very frustrated big game hunter.

Most of us know that simple, round lead balls were historically used as projectiles, and these eventually gave way to cores of lead cased in copper jackets. Of the latter, a couple of types were available to John: one that expanded too quickly and failed to penetrate and one with tremendous penetration but minimum expansion. In back-to-back hunting years, Nosler had experienced both types of bullet failure. He knew that if he was going to continue enjoying his hobby of big game hunting using his new high-velocity rifle, he needed to create a bullet that was completely different from

John Nosler, a bullet designer, in 1950s Ashland. *Gary Lewis Outdoor collection.*

anything available at the time. He only wanted to create bullets that he and his hunting buddies could use each season while he continued to run his expanding agricultural trucking business.

John Nosler didn't have an engineering degree—in fact, he had no degree at all. What he brought to the task of creating bullets was a young lifetime of mechanical experimentation and hands-on experience from living on a California ranch. Growing up, he learned that, if something was broken, you had to fix it with whatever was available. He had always worked on cars and had even built hotrod racecars from Ford Model Ts and Model As. At the age of nineteen, Nosler developed a counterbalance system for the Model A crankshaft that the Ford Motor Company adopted. Ford was so impressed with Nosler's skills that the company offered to send him to engineering school, after which he would become a full-time Ford engineer. But instead of taking the offer, John and his wife, Louise, and their two-month-old son headed to Reedsport, Oregon, in a Model A Ford coupe, to take over a small Ford dealership that the company had offered to him.

While Nosler was initially quite successful at selling cars, the crush of the Great Depression in the 1930s resulted in a large amount of defaults on the cars that John had sold, mostly to the employees of the local failing sawmills. Once he was able to unload the dealership, John and his family headed to Ashland, where John's brother and cousin lived and where John had heard that the deer hunting was excellent. Before leaving, John purchased a truck off the Reedsport sales floor for the drive to Ashland.

Once he arrived in Ashland, John's cousin decided to join him in a produce business that hauled fruits and vegetables from California to Oregon—Nosler Produce was born. The men would drive to San Francisco and the area's surrounding farmers' markets, and they would truck the goods back to Oregon stores. Along the way, John bought one of the first Peterbilt Cummins diesel trucks that was built for highway use. The business prospered, and John ended up with a small fleet of Peterbilt trucks and trailers. The business also provided him some spare time for hunting and competitively shooting with the Ashland Gun Club. Later, John organized a shooting club in the basement of the National Guard Armory on Oak Street. John was finally able to hunt the black-tail deer that he had heard so much about before moving to Ashland, and he got his first trophy off Green Springs Road, just east of town. Emboldened by the successful deer hunting around Ashland, John became interested in going after bigger game, which soon changed everything.

With government contracts for produce during World War II, John's business thrived, and he was able to go moose hunting in British Columbia, fulfilling a longtime dream. However, the hunt ended in frustration. The bullets that were available to hunters in the 1940s had not kept up with the era's newer, higher-velocity rifles. John thought that, surely, someone would build a bullet with a balance of penetration and expansion. But after the 1946 moose season, John spent the winter at his drawing board and, later, in his truck garage, handmaking a duel-core bullet that he and his friends could try out next season. He called his creations "partition jacket bullets."

Nosler at work in his Ashland shop, handmaking a new bullet design. *Gary Lewis Outdoor collection.*

What he had sketched was a partition separating two bullets—the front part was made to expand, and the rear part was made to penetrate. Even though they were roughly made, the partition bullets worked amazingly well during a September 1947 trip to Canada. Both John and his friend Clarence Purdy, a shooting supply dealer, only needed one shot to take down a moose with the new bullets—two shots, two moose.

But even with such great success, Nosler didn't intend to go into the bullet business. He continued to test them, but someone else always had to make them. John eventually wanted to see the partition bullets made available on the market, and he sought a buyer for his idea. After approaching a number of other companies without success, Nosler presented his design to the Winchester Company in Connecticut, but this didn't work out either. Winchester engineers found the new design odd and very different. Their current machines couldn't make it and new setups would be too costly to make a profit. Finally, John decided to go back home to his Ashland garage and build the machinery he needed to make the bullets himself. He formally patented his design and incorporated the Nosler Partition Bullet Company in 1948.

Every free moment John spent studying engineering manuals, designing equipment and testing bullets; he had to learn how he could make them faster than he could by hand. For everything to work, the trucking company had to be sold so that John and his family could build bullets full time. They put both their life savings and the money from the sale into the new business—they were all in. For many of the early years, John, Louise and their son Ron worked in every phase of the bullet business. John was the engineer and designer, marketing man and the purchasing manager of all the raw materials they needed. Louise worked alongside John in the shop when she wasn't busy as the office manager, filling orders and handling paperwork. After school, Ron ran the shop's handpress.

By the mid-1950s, Nosler Partition Bullet Company needed to expand. Starting with five acres at 382 Wightman Street, near the local college, John had previously donated the southern two and a half acres of his property to Southern Oregon State College (Southern Oregon University today) so that the school could build a football field and gym. He did this as a favor for his friend and the college's president Stevenson, whom John met while serving on the Ashland City Council. Aside from this generosity, the expansion of a bullet factory in a residential area didn't appeal to city decision-makers, so Nosler began to wonder if he needed to take his business elsewhere. William Dawkins, an Ashland writer, wrote a feature article about Nosler bullets that appeared in the *Oregonian* in 1956.

!! THANKS !!

Your orders and good letters commending our product convinced us you are looking for the best in bullets for big game hunting. Heavy demand for 150 and 180 gr. in 30 caliber has delayed production of other cal. & weights. Attention Elk Hunters: **THIS BULLET IS DOING A WHALE OF A JOB THIS SEASON!**

•

NOSLER PARTITION JACKET BULLET

John A. Nosler   382 Weightman St.   Ashland, Oregon

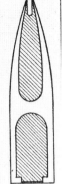

One of John Nosler's original Ashland advertisements for his new bullet design. *Gary Lewis Outdoor collection.*

At the same time, the town of Bend in Central Oregon was actively recruiting small businesses to relocate there. Since central Oregon was one of John's favorite hunting locales, the offer to move his business there was very attractive. Bend went all out for the Noslers; the town gave them acreage for a new factory and sent truck rigs to Ashland to haul all of John's equipment at no cost to him. Bend merchants also donated their time and supplies to help make the move as seamless as possible for the Noslers. So, John sold his remaining Ashland property, including his home, shop and truck garage, to Southern Oregon University.

Seventy-two years after the invention of the partition jacket bullet, it is still in production and is still a favorite of big game hunters worldwide. It is now offered in fourteen different calibers. The company that John Nosler started in Ashland, Oregon, as a way to have higher-quality bullets is now based in Bend and nearby Redmond, Oregon. John passed away in 2010, at the age of ninety-seven. His son Bob, who purchased the company when his father retired in 1988, is now a chairman of the company's board. John's grandson and namesake is the current president of the extremely successful family-owned business. Meanwhile, the Noslers' former Ashland property on Wightman Street, the site of the partition bullet's origin, is currently occupied by Southern Oregon University's campus public safety office and motor pool.

For a more complete discussion of John Nosler's life and work, please read the 2005 publication *John Nosler: Going Ballistic* by John Nosler, as told to Gary Lewis. The book contains a detailed account of John's life, complete with one hundred photos.

6

THE LITTLE AUTO DEALERSHIP
THAT COULD!

How did one small Chrysler-Plymouth dealership in post–World War II Ashland,
Oregon, become a national powerhouse, with stores that reach across America?

Out on highway 99, near the Red Barn Auction House, on one
September evening in 1968, a car-pedestrian accident occurred
that changed everything. Walt "Tex" DeBoer, the owner of
Ashland's Lithia Chrysler dealership near the Plaza, died within a week
of the accident—he had never regained consciousness. DeBoer was fifty-
seven years old. While Walt's death was tragic enough for his family, shortly
thereafter, the Chrysler Corporation issued a nonrenewable two-year
franchise, and the family's twenty-two-year-old business was given two years
to liquidate as a Dodge-only franchise.

Americans' pent-up desire to once again purchase an automobile after
World War II was enormous. Walt De Boer secured an automobile franchise
in 1946, shortly after moving to Ashland, from Eugene, and he named the
dealership after Ashland's famous Lithia water. Between 1946 and 1955, the
automobile industry's production of new vehicles quadrupled annually. With
the passing of the 1956 New Highway Act, all parts of the country were
eventually linked with interstate highways. As a result, one in six working
Americans became directly or indirectly linked to the automobile industry,
as the United States became the world's largest manufacturer of cars.

At the age of twenty-one, in 1964, Sid DeBoer, the oldest of Walt's
six children, joined the family business as its full-time bookkeeper and

Walt DeBoer's original Ashland dealership. *Courtesy of Lithia Auto Stores.*

office manager. Even as a young child, Sid had worked at the dealership, straightening the front row of cars in the lot. "Dad would let me do that." DeBoer exclaimed, "I could drive when I was seven years old!" Upon his father's death, Sid, at the age of twenty-five, assumed full control of the soon-to-be-terminated dealership. "That very month, I sold thirty-five cars all by myself. I was the only employee. Sometimes, you can get stronger from tragedy" recalled DeBoer.

The following year, Dick Heimann, a factory representative for Chrysler, was sent to Ashland to work out the final dealer agreement with Sid. In an interesting twist, Heimann was able to help DeBoer get a permanent franchise in the adjoining town of Medford to replace the Ashland store. DeBoer soon offered Heimann an opportunity to come to work as a partner in the new Medford store, and the former factory representative accepted. The relationship between the two thrived; as Sid explained, "We sold so many Dodges in Medford when we first started, we didn't know how good we were." However, they had yet to learn how to make money in the car business. The debt from the purchase of the Medford store was significant. "Initially, we were only trying to survive with big loan payments." A Chrysler Corporation representative once spent two weeks in town, helping DeBoer and Heimann see how holding each department accountable for its costs and profits was superior to spreading gross figures across the store. After some initial success, the pair acquired additional stores, and by 1987, they had a total of five dealerships in Medford and Grants Pass through leveraging equity.

At this time, the partners were introduced to a new concept called "public dealerships," which they used to raise their company's capital. In order for their public dealerships to work, the pair had to convince Wall Street investors that their car dealership groups were viable stock opportunities. This was a hard sell because they had to promise rapid growth, and there were few stock market analysts who knew about the car business—some didn't even have cars of their own. Major automakers weren't crazy about the idea either, as they preferred to have individuals in charge of their dealerships rather than shareholders. Yet, taking the business public still seemed to be a better way for the business to grow, as it allowed DeBoer and Heimann to avoid substantial bank debt and months of negotiations. Besides, changes were occurring in the automobile industry; large dealership groups were rapidly replacing small, independent dealers, and profit margins were tightening. An obvious additional benefit to having more retail stores was that companies increased their economies of scale.

The idea of raising capital through an initial public offering (IPO) never left DeBoer's mind, but it didn't actually happen until December 1996. Armed with the details of a multifaceted operating model, the pair went on a two-week, twenty-city, fifty-presentation road show, traveling by commercial aircraft to persuade investors. The $27 million that was raised allowed Lithia to develop an aggressive growth plan, advancing from five stores to forty-one stores in three short years. Today, it is not possible to overstate the importance of DeBoer's vison and dogged determination to find a better way to grow his business.

Rural and small-town dealerships that were underperforming initially became the pair's acquisition targets, as they were familiar to partners DeBoer and Heimann. A team was created by Lithia to evaluate dealerships as they became available, making sure that the company was only buying underachievers, not broken stores that were beyond fixing; the

Sid DeBoer, who took Lithia Motors public in 1996. *Courtesy of Lithia Auto Stores.*

company was not interested in dealerships whose owners were not ready to sell or whose geographic area was already saturated. The team's task was to find any identifiable reason that a dealership was not as successful as it should be and make a judgment of whether it could be improved. For example, perhaps the previous owner had not maximized some areas of their business that they should have.

After a dealership was purchased, Lithia would apply its standardized operating formula, which had worked in existing stores, to its business model, bringing it into alignment with the other dealerships, thereby creating a common culture. As a minimum requirement, new acquisitions were not allowed to reopen as Lithia stores until ten-minute credit checks; thirty-minute trade-in appraisals; ninety-minute sales transactions; sixty-day, or three-thousand-mile, used car warranties; mission statements for each department; and management information systems had been put in place. The information systems made it possible to track the daily sales, inventories and profits of every dealership. All of this, coupled with a continuing efficiency model, is how Lithia seems to drive a common culture. The company's mantra is "If someone else has done it, you can do it."

The company's methodical plan of aggressive growth has resulted in a kind of inspirational lesson; this tiny business, which was tucked away in southern Oregon, became the third-largest automobile group in the country. Mirroring its Medford Auto Mall concept, Lithia has started to acquire auto groups, not just individual dealerships; in doing this, the business has maintained its goal of significant expansion every year and has encouraged a more decentralized decision-making model. Lithia's recent acquisitions have extended its brand into New York, Vermont, New Jersey, Florida, Massachusetts and Pennsylvania, making it not only the third-largest auto dealership by sales but also the most complete coast-to-coast auto network. With fifteen thousand employees, Lithia Auto Stores can now be found in twenty states, selling thirty brands of cars and trucks at nearly two hundred dealerships. Lithia ranks in at 265 on the *Forbes* Fortune 500 list.

Just as Sid joined his father in the automobile business, Sid's son Bryan DeBoer now serves as Lithia's chief operating officer (CEO), and his son Mark serves as the company's vice-president for corporate development. Bryan has been credited with the creation of the accelerated acquisition growth model that has been responsible for the addition of several large auto groups to the company in recent years. Lithia Motors has come a long way since Bryan and Mark's grandfather established the company in 1946. However, judging by the activities of the family foundation, the DeBoers

Lithia Auto Stores' state-of-the-art headquarters in Medford, Oregon. *Courtesy of Lithia Auto Stores.*

have taken countless opportunities to give back to the community in which it all started. The family gives millions of dollars annually; a few of their more recent and readily identifiable contributions have gone to Southern Oregon University's athletic pavilion, Mount Ashland's ski lodge and the Ashland YMCA's restoration of a former Girl Scout camp at Lake of the Woods. As Sid DeBoer explains, "Our family intends to leave a large endowment because a number of important things won't happen without it."

PART IV
POLITICS

7

An Illegitimate President? Not a Concern in Republican Ashland

It may come as a shock to contemporary Ashlanders, but there once was a time when the town was solidly Republican.

In the interest of reuniting the country, which was still divided several years after the Civil War, President Rutherford Hayes traveled for thousands of miles to Oregon in an attempt to strengthen the state's allegiance to the Union. He was aware of the ongoing reports that, throughout the war, Oregon and California sought to form an independent Pacific Republic. Hayes admired how his hero, George Washington, had traveled to all thirteen states as president and saw a western trip as his own opportunity to shore up relations with the far-western states.

Oddly, despite Hayes's desire to restore harmony, it was his election that divided the country once more. Democrats said he stole the national election by benefiting from the two sets of vote counts sent by Florida, South Carolina, Louisiana and Oregon. It was charged that a partisan-appointed commission negated a sizable popular vote victory for his opponent, Democratic New York governor Samuel Tilden. Throughout the four years of his presidency, Rutherford was referred to by Democrats as "Rutherfraud" or simply "His Fraudulency." Clearly, a cloud hung over the president's administration. He had lost the popular vote by a whopping 250,000 votes, and when Congress appointed a partisan electoral commission, all 20 of the disputed votes from the four states in question, including Oregon, were awarded to Hayes. This gave Hayes 185 electoral votes, just 1 more than his

President Hayes, the first sitting president to visit Ashland. *Author's collection.*

opponent, and the presidency. But there was more; the terms of a friendly agreement soon surfaced, whereby Hayes's administration agreed to several southern concessions, including ending the military occupation of the South and appointing a southerner to a cabinet position. In return, the South's attempts to block Hayes from the White House would end. Rank-and-file Democrats cried "fraud."

However, none of these accusations seemed to matter in the mostly Republican-voting town of Ashland or in any way dampened the town's much anticipated chance to see an American president in the flesh. Hayes was traveling north from Redding, by stagecoach, with the first lady, and they arrived at the Ashland Plaza on the afternoon of September 27, 1880. General William Tecumseh Sherman accompanied the presidential party, riding "shotgun" atop the stagecoach, to protect the president from the notorious bandit Black Bart, who regularly held up coaches on the stage line between California and Oregon. The president's six-horse coach arrived in Ashland without incident, and he triumphantly entered town to the sound of pealing church bells and countless hurrahs—it was electric. A local newspaper reporter gushed about the arrival of a president from three thousand miles away, asserting that time and distance had surely been annihilated.

For the next hour Hayes belonged to Ashland's 800 residents and an estimated 1,200 others who eagerly surrounded the newly built platform at the base of the town flagpole. However, only a week before the president's appearance, Oregon Democratic senator James Slater reminded a large Ashland audience that the previous election had been a huge fraud. Everyone, the senator asserted, knew that Democrat Samuel Tilden was the person who was really elected. But despite the nagging questions of Hayes's legitimacy, the *Ashland Tidings* urged its readers to honor the president and set aside petty partisanship. Judging by the reception in the plaza, more folks in Ashland agreed with the *Tidings*'s editorial comments than the senator's. Ashland's crowds seemed delighted to greet both the president and the two other famous individuals who accompanied him—the First Lady, nicknamed "Lemonade Lucy" and General Sherman.

Lucy Hayes had a national following among those who supported Prohibition, and she had plenty of local supporters in Ashland, a town with a reputation for keeping saloons out. The town's motto, "Industry, Education, Temperance—Ashland Honors Those Who Foster These," was clearly stated on the newly erected welcoming arch, where the president and First Lady stood. Within a year of Lucy's visit, the Ashland Woman's Christian Temperance Association led a war against saloons, forcing at least one to close its doors and its owner to flee to a more welcoming town. But not everyone shared Lucy's enthusiasm for temperance—not even everyone within the president's administration. When asked about the president's dry state dinners, one cabinet member commented, dryly, that the water flowed like champagne.

The other popular traveling companion of the president was the legendary, sixty-year-old Civil War general William Tecumseh Sherman, who, at the time, was serving as the commander of the U.S. Army. Veterans of the Grand Army of the Republic (GAR) were in abundance in Ashland's crowd; they had come to cheer for their hero at the Monday afternoon festivities. Both the president and the general spoke briefly before they were presented with a tray of homegrown fruit donated by local orchardist Orlando Coolidge. Much handshaking and applause followed both of their speeches.

While this may have been Ashland's first experience of hosting a president, it was the second time that Jimmy McLaughlin, the town's oldest citizen at the age of ninety-three, had shaken the hand of a president—or so he claimed. McLaughlin was given a seat of honor on the reception platform and had the privilege of shaking the hand of Hayes. McLaughlin reminisced that, at the age of six or eight, he had also shaken hands with then-president George Washington while he was living in Philadelphia. Whether this was an idle boast or not, the fact that Jimmy McLaughlin's claim was mathematically possible meant that the Ashlander's life had actually encompassed the term of every American president (nineteen in all) to date.

Ashland officials telegraphed the leaders of the nearby town of Jacksonville to let them know the time of the president's departure so that they could have a welcoming celebration ready (President Hayes was to spend the night at the U.S. Hotel in Jacksonville). But, apparently, no advance men paved the way for presidential visits in 1880. Clearly, no one had researched the town's political leanings, or Jacksonville would have been removed as Hayes's next stop. Even the town's newspapers should have given pause to such a controversial Republican administration; the *Democratic Times* had been particularly vicious in its attacks on the president in the month before his arrival. The paper urged its readers to abstain from any recognition of Hayes as president. The heavily Democratic town council had no reception in place when the presidential stagecoach arrived shortly after 6:00 p.m. that evening.

Nevertheless, some of the folks in Jacksonville managed to pull together the town band for some patriotic music, and numerous individuals welcomed the presidential party as it arrived at the U.S. Hotel. General Sherman, in an effort to deflect the political slight of town officials, told the crowd that he and the president really preferred the spontaneous greeting of the people to a formal ceremony. The town's slight, however, would not go unnoticed nationally, as several papers commented on Jacksonville's failure to properly acknowledge a sitting president.

Several sitting presidents would stop for a visit in Ashland in the future, but advancements in transportation technology drastically changed the way in which Ashlanders greeted visiting presidents. If the townspeople of Ashland wanted to get a glimpse of another visiting president, they had to gather at the railroad depot, several blocks from the plaza, where they had enthusiastically welcomed their first and most controversial presidential visitor.

8

A PARTY FOR TEDDY WITHOUT THE GUEST OF HONOR

On the night of President Roosevelt's visit, 125 well-dressed couples showed up for a presidential ball. The celebration stretched well into the next morning. Teddy Roosevelt, however, couldn't make it.

In a little over thirty years, the tiny town of Ashland hosted as many as five sitting U.S. presidents. Why? Why was this small town such a magnet for presidents? The answer can be found just beyond A Street, in Ashland's formerly bustling railroad district. Strategically located near the Oregon-California border, at the base of the steep Siskiyou Mountains, Ashland was a required stop for trains traveling both north and south. The Southern Pacific Railroad built a train yard with a roundhouse in Ashland so that engines could be added or subtracted as needed. A large depot was constructed at a site that could be reached by a short walk down Fourth Street.

This depot made it possible for Ashlanders to see and hear Teddy Roosevelt, as well as Benjamin Harrison, William Howard Taft, Woodrow Wilson and Warren Harding, in the flesh while the "presidential special" trains were readied for their next destinations on Pacific Coast tours. This stop also provided traveling presidents the almost irresistible opportunity to speak to residents out of the back of their train cars. In the spring of 1903, local, progressive Republicans welcomed the opportunity to see and hear a living legend—the Rough Rider himself—Teddy Roosevelt.

The entire town was giddy in anticipation of Roosevelt's visit—even though he couldn't stay long. Nothing was left to chance, including an elaborately orchestrated "Welcome to Oregon" reception. The prominent citizens of Ashland planned a glitzy, formal-dress presidential ball in the Ganiard Opera House for the night of Roosevelt's visit and talk. A full two days before his arrival, the *Ashland Tidings* made sure that everyone in the town was briefed on the soon-to-be forty-five-year-old president. Readers were informed as to how to pronounce his last name (with three syllables), that he had no gray hair, that pictures of him don't do him justice (his teeth are large, and his whole body moved when he gave a speech), that he enunciated with an accent (not wars but "waahs") and that he would be accompanied by six Secret Service

President Teddy Roosevelt stopping in Ashland during his 1904 campaign swing. *Author's collection.*

agents, dressed in tall hats and long coats, who are along for his protection.

An enormous arch, which was tall enough—at thirty-four feet—to easily fit a locomotive under it, was erected over the main track, just a few feet from where the golden spike of 1887 had been driven into the line to celebrate the connection of Oregon and California, which had completed the final link of a railroad circle around the United States. Unfortunately, though, at some point during the festivities, the town's American flag and Oregon grape–draped structure fell, bringing its top piece (a stuffed Oregon mountain lion) and huge pictures of the president crashing to the ground.

In addition to the arch, telegraph poles, railroad water tanks and depot buildings had been decked out in red, white and blue. Souvenir picture booklets of Ashland and the surrounding area were prepared as gifts to the president and his party on behalf of the city. And a local drugstore, McNair Brothers, offered portraits of Roosevelt for twenty-five cents each. A cannon that was located on Chautauqua Butte, the current site of the Oregon Shakespeare Festival, was prepared to fire a salute as the president's train pulled in. Even the seating area for onlookers was organized, with some getting "places of honor" near the rear of the train, where the president would give his speech. Schoolchildren, college students from the Normal School, veterans of the Grand Army of the Republic (former union soldiers

The 1904 Republican candidate's campaign pins. *Author's collection.*

in uniform) and national guardsmen were all given choice spots. Glimpsing the president would not have been easy without a priority position in the crowd, which was estimated to number six thousand people. But it appears that no one was disappointed.

Roosevelt captivated his huge audience with a prepared stump speech delivered in his typical, animated manner. He specifically addressed the delegation of Union veterans and complemented them on their courage, which held the country together. Without them, he said, a president would not be able to travel from the Atlantic to the Pacific under the American flag. Characteristically, Roosevelt's speech turned to his own exploits; the former lieutenant general of the rough riders said that he and his contemporaries also possessed that American fighting spirit but that there just wasn't enough war to go around. Even though it was a smaller war, Roosevelt explained that the Spanish-American War opened the United States to the Pacific and gave it a presence in world affairs.

An enthusiastic Roosevelt supporter in the depot crowd displayed a banner that read: "Hurrah for the man who does things." This banner provided Roosevelt a perfect opportunity to heap praise on Oregon's early founders. Pointing to the banner, Roosevelt said that the men who founded Oregon were "men who did things." While the comment is perhaps odd-sounding today, a raucous "hurrahing" punctuated each comment Roosevelt made. The president invoked Abraham Lincoln's name and

Ashland's Ganiard Opera House, where a presidential ball was held in conjunction with Teddy Roosevelt's visit. *Courtesy of the Terry Skibby collection.*

showered further praise on those who had fought for their nation, and he warned that there was a need for men to be hardy and rugged, rather than gentle and mild.

At the conclusion of his speech, Roosevelt was off, apologizing that he could not extend his short visit any longer. As the train slowly pulled out of Ashland, with the president bowing to the assembly, children gave him flowers, and the town band struck up "America." The crowd sang along with the thousands of copies of the lyrics that had been carefully handed out in advance of Roosevelt's arrival. But what about the much-anticipated presidential ball that had been set for later that evening? It, too, was reported to have been a tremendous success, even without its guest of honor. It was reported that 125 couples danced and celebrated, not leaving the town opera house until well after sunrise the next morning.

9

TAKE "TAINTED ROBBER-BARON MONEY" FOR A LIBRARY?

Why would any town not take "free" money to build a library? The Carnegie library donations of the early 1900s are well-known; what's less commonly known is how many towns turned down Andrew Carnegie's money. At least two members of the Ashland City Council opposed accepting the funds and indicated that they spoke for many people; they were not interested in "worshipping at the Carnegie shrine" at the public's expense. In nearby Medford, the local paper consistently ran editorials against the man, who, they accused, made his money by exploiting his workers and who, they said, was worse than former slave owners. Others were also appalled by Carnegie's use of child labor in his mills. Despite the fact that steel baron Andrew Carnegie paid for 1,689 public library buildings in the United States, including 31 in Oregon, opposition to his generous gifts continued throughout the construction initiative. Nearly fifty communities rejected a Carnegie grant by either a city council vote or popular election, which are overt expressions of local opposition. Why? What explains this trend of walking away from such a significant gift?

Often, the unwillingness of these towns reflected a belief that paralleled the concern of Ashland's two opposing council members—that Carnegie was building memorials to himself. There were additional objections, however, in towns throughout the United States. One concern that many towns had was that Carnegie was only paying for the structure, not the books, furniture, staff salaries or annual upkeep costs that were required to maintain a library. These ongoing costs had to be alleviated through a tax on the public, according to Carnegie's conditions. Then, there was the "tainted money" argument. This perception came from Carnegie's reputation as a brutal exploiter of his steelworkers, as personified by the Homestead, Pennsylvania strike, where armed strikebreakers were used to attack and kill those who were trying to form a union. His company was responsible for shooting those who were on strike for better conditions and pay, and this came at a time when Carnegie was simultaneously preaching how the wealthy should be working to "lift up" the working man.

In other communities that were seeking Carnegie funds, local battles played out over the fact that building sites needed to exist in order to receive a grant. This became a rather drawn-out issue in Ashland, and it was a much larger obstacle for the town to overcome in its push to secure a library building than the "tainted money" argument. Several sites were proposed, but the library board was unanimous in its recommendation to put it at the newly renovated entrance of Lithia Park, where an old flour mill once stood. There would be no cost for the land, as the city already owned the park. However, many others argued that the property flooded and was, at best, a wet area where no basement could be built. Others said that a library building there would obscure the park itself.

Those who lived on and owned property east of the downtown plaza raised money to buy a corner lot at Gresham and Main Streets as a location for the new library, as they suggested that downtown had become stagnant. Their proposed site was available for $3,500, and they had already raised half of the needed funds. Many other sites were suggested, including one on North Main Street that came complete with a bell to welcome visitors coming into town by train. Yet another idea was to place the library on Granite Street; besides being the most beautiful street in town, it was pointed out that, when an electric car line is built to run up the street to Mount Ashland, people going up the street in the morning could stop and check out some books for the day and drop them off on the way home. Those who favored the old mill site accused the Eastsiders of simply trying to inflate their property values by having a library nearby.

Soon, city councilmembers weighed in; the majority of them openly rejected what was now called the park site. The park commission indicated that they were resolute in their opposition to the use of the park property for any use other than that of a park. This left the council with the task of designing a ballot that reflected the popular will of the town and what they thought was best. Two sites, including the park site and the Gresham Street property, were listed on a ballot and voted on in a special election. No

Ashland's original 1912 Carnegie Library. *Courtesy of Southern Oregon Historical Society.*

other locations were listed, and it was generally assumed that the park site would win handily, judging by the local talk and numerous volatile "letters to the editor." Surprisingly, the voter turnout was low after all of the ongoing controversy, and those who did cast ballots did so overwhelmingly for the Gresham Street corner location.

The decision to finally accept a Carnegie library was less surprising. Ashland saw itself as a progressive town and hosted a Chautauqua each summer; it also had had both an opera house and a college. A formal library building was something for the town to be proud of, because it made a visual statement about the culture of Ashland. Once the "tainted money" concerns died down, the real battle in Ashland was over the library's location. Bitter at times, the one councilmember who held out explained that his "no" vote on the establishing ordinance was a protest for how few sites had been explored.

Carnegie viewed his library grants as a kind of a bribe to get towns to support their own best interests. He was only providing the shell that towns had to fill. He wanted to be remembered for what he had coaxed others to do, and it seemed to work. The vast majority of communities enthusiastically embraced Andrew Carnegie's library program, which included taxing themselves for future costs, buying books and furniture and providing a building site. Despite some initial reluctance, both Ashland and Medford opened their Carnegie library doors to the public in 1912.

10

From Southern Oregon College to the White House

Locked in a tight race to win the 1960 Democratic Party nomination, Senator John Kennedy had to defeat Oregon's enormously popular "favorite son," making Ashland's small college an important stop.

A defeat in Oregon could have been fatal to Senator Kennedy's campaign. John F. Kennedy, whose Catholic religion was a concern, needed to win this overwhelmingly Protestant state. The state's college campuses had, thus far, been friendly territories for the witty, youthful candidate, and Southern Oregon College's gym promised to be the same, especially since his speech was preceded by a glowing introduction from a popular campus professor.

Kennedy, himself, saw the Oregon primary as, likely, the most important in the country when it came to his chances of securing the Democratic nomination. It wasn't the state's small number of delegates that Kennedy was really after; he knew that the psychological lift from winning a majority in Oregon would be vital—it would be an impression of inevitability. He knew a "Stop Kennedy" movement was afoot around Oregon's extremely popular senior senator Wayne Morse, whose slogan, "The Candidate who votes the way he talks," was well known in the state. Both Morse and the state of Oregon had a proud reputation of being political mavericks. Even before the formal announcement of his candidacy for the presidency, on January 2, 1960, Massachusetts senator Kennedy made five trips to Far-West Oregon in 1959. During the previous tour, he attended the Oregon

Campaign pins for Senators Kennedy and Morse, who were competing for the 1960 Democratic nomination in Oregon. *Author's collection.*

Statehood Centennial Exposition and visited Eugene, Salem, Seaside and Portland. The senator had never lost an election in his life, and this kind of advance work may have been the reason why.

Meanwhile, Senator Wayne Morse was counting on a deadlocked convention, where his anticipated delegates would become bargaining chips and he would hopefully be given the vice-presidency. Morse also had committees working for him in several additional states. Kennedy expressed to the press that he thought it would be difficult to beat Morse in Oregon because he was a "favorite son" of the state; he went so far as to say that he hoped for a strong second place. Five candidates were listed on the Democratic ballot, including Hubert Humphrey, Lyndon Johnson, John Kennedy, Wayne Morse and Stuart Symington. A candidate who was not on the ballot but was still a favorite of many was Adlai Stevenson; he indicated that, if Kennedy won Oregon, he deserved the nomination.

Aside from Morse's stature in the state, Kennedy had at least two other concerns when it came to him winning in Oregon. First, he was a known Catholic running in a heavily Protestant state. Some voters thought that a Catholic president's loyalty to the pope might overshadow his loyalty to America. Kennedy's Catholic faith was a difficult obstacle for voters in 1960 America. Would a Catholic president take orders from the Vatican?

Senator John Kennedy deplaning at Medford Airport before his appearance at Southern Oregon College in 1960. *Courtesy of Southern Oregon Historical Society.*

Second, Kennedy's brother's work against the mobsters in the Teamsters Union, which included the indictment of Portland's popular Democratic mayor upset a lot of workers in Oregon. Kennedy knew that a majority win in Oregon might erase the religious issue, end the "Stop Kennedy" drive, and all but secure the nomination for him—it would be his eighth straight primary win.

It was this intimidating political environment that the Massachusetts senator and his campaign aide, Pierre Salinger, landed in one Saturday morning in April 1960. The men were picked up from the Medford Airport and driven to Ashland for a reception and a speech. Later, Kennedy served as the grand marshal of Medford's Pear Blossom Parade in a late model convertible; Medford businessman Wally Watkins agreed to be Kennedy's chauffeur. Watkins was a self-proclaimed Democrat with the perfect car, a cream-colored 1959 Lincoln convertible.

Kennedy's first stop in Ashland was at a small coffee hour at 445 Liberty Street, the recently acquired home of Dr. Arthur Kreisman. Between 9:45

and 10:45, almost three hundred Ashlanders descended on the Kreisman house and backyard, just up from Triangle Park, to meet the Democratic front-runner. Understandably overwhelmed, the Kreismans were fortunate to have the help of both the Ashland League of Women Voters and an unusually large living room. Professor Kreisman, who was also born in Massachusetts, had extended the initial invitation for Kennedy to speak at the college. Long involved in party politics, Dr. Kreisman had previously hosted Adlai Stevenson and Estes Kefauver. This time, however, a fellow New Englander was the candidate, and he admitted to some favoritism, even though he despised Joe Kennedy, the candidate's father.

Even the best-laid plans from Kennedy's traveling campaign aides, Pierre Salinger and his younger brother, Ted Kennedy, couldn't fix one problem though: the candidate was suffering from a throbbing sore throat and was in need of medical attention before the scheduled 11:00 a.m. college speech. Art Kreisman's personal physician, Harvey Woods, came to the rescue. After a quick look down the future president's throat, Dr. Woods prescribed some relief. During the coffee hour, it also seemed that Salinger was dropping his ashes all over the Kreismans' carpets as he incessantly paced back and forth, making countless long-distance phone calls. The college professor could see his entire paycheck going to cover the cost of those calls and a new carpet, but much to his relief, the phone bill was later paid for by the Kennedy campaign, and Salinger's cigar ashes were easily vacuumed up. Kreisman was so preoccupied throughout the day, with the reception, his introductory speech, Kennedy's sore throat and Pierre Salinger's cigar ashes, that he didn't recall much from Kennedy's campus address.

On a rainy Friday in May, sixty years before the writing of this book, Senator Kennedy's fears were proven to be unfounded, as he won yet another decisive victory over the entire field of Democratic candidates. Morse promptly dropped out of the race. Ashland's vote paralleled statewide returns. Morse was a distant second to Kennedy, who captured a 50.9 percent majority of all votes cast. Clearly, Ashland and Southern Oregon College had a brief, but memorable and historic moment on one April day in 1960.

PART V
WHY HERE?

II

What Was the U.S. Liberty Bell Doing in Ashland, Oregon?

Thousands left their beds at 3:00 a.m. to see the bell strapped to a railroad car.

The night of July 16, 1915, may have been the noisiest night in Ashland history. According to the July 15, 1915 edition of *Ashland Tidings*, an enormous—if sleepy—crowd, with whistles, bells and fireworks, was planning to gather in the town at 2:00 a.m. the next day for the rare chance to view one of the most prized relics of American history. Other than Fort McHenry's "Star-Spangled Banner" flag, it is difficult to imagine a more revered American icon than the Liberty Bell, which is held today in the secure custody of Philadelphia's Liberty Bell Center. So, why does the Southern Oregon Historical Society have, in its collection, a July 16, 1915 picture of the bell strapped to a gondola car at the Ashland Depot? Ashland is nearly three thousand miles away from the bell's home in Philadelphia. Even more intriguing is that the obviously nighttime picture was snapped at 3:00 a.m.! Here is a local history mystery embedded in American politics from over one hundred years ago.

Who would advocate that this fragile, cracked symbol be transported all the way to the West Coast by rail? Philadelphia city officials loudly opposed the idea, yet the trip was endorsed by former president Teddy Roosevelt, sitting president Woodrow Wilson, five hundred thousand schoolchildren, San Francisco mayor James Rolph and other ordinary Americans who were shocked by the May 7, 1915 sinking of the *Lusitania*. Besides the obvious potential physical damage that could have befallen the bell, many

The Liberty Bell, strapped to a train car, arrived in Ashland at 3:00 a.m., but it still drew a huge crowd. *Photograph courtesy of Terry Skibby.*

thought that the proposed trip, which was to end at the Panama-Pacific Exposition, was disrespectful. After all, fairs connote livestock pens and food booths; clearly, the symbol of freedom belonged on permanent display in Philadelphia, not ingloriously strapped to a railroad car for a bumpy road trip to yet another fair. Debates over the trip continued, even though both Roosevelt and Wilson argued that the appearance of the Liberty Bell Special, as the tour was called, would enhance Americans' patriotism at a time when they needed it most. After years of unassimilated immigration from Eastern Europe and war clouds abroad, this seemed to be the right time to remind Americans of their shared heritage and love of country.

Playing a classic booster role, Mayor James Rolph of San Francisco lobbied heavily for the trip once his city was selected as the location for the first American World Fair on the faraway West Coast. He maintained that the appearance of the Liberty Bell would help westerners identify with America's European beginnings. Organized by San Francisco teachers, thousands of California schoolchildren joined the mayor's effort by writing letters to Philadelphia officials, urging them to allow a visit from the Liberty Bell. Back in Philadelphia, however, no plans or funding were forthcoming. Most city officials still opposed any movement of the priceless national treasure. Only a stunning attack at sea and the deaths of more than one hundred American citizens could have temporarily wrestled the icon away from Philadelphia. In early May 1915, Germany's sinking of the English ship *Lusitania* caused Philadelphia's leaders to re-examine their opposition, as the need to unite the nation took on a new urgency.

With great haste, and no previous planning by the Pennsylvania Railroad, a route for the bell was put together across the Midwest and through the Pacific Northwest, culminating in San Francisco. The return trip would follow a southern and northeastern pattern. There were 175 stops scheduled for the bell after it left Philadelphia on July 5, 1915. A specially cushioned car carried the valuable relic, which many viewers reported to be a surprisingly smallish-looking worn bell. Powered by a generator, stage lights kept the bell aglow for night viewing.

Regardless of its size, the Liberty Bell was a wildly popular attraction; tens of thousands of Americans were eager to touch, kiss and have their photos taken beside it. Philadelphia police officers who were assigned to protect the bell quickly gave up any hope of keeping folks at a distance from it once the train came to a stop in each town. The published list of towns and cities that the bell visited in Oregon did not include any stops south of Roseburg. So, how does one account for the photograph of the bell in Ashland when no stop was scheduled there? The answer appears to be linked to Oregon senator Chamberlain. Once the cross-country route was announced, as many as one hundred town mayors begged their elected officials to secure a stop in their town, even if it had to be a short one. A note from Roseburg indicated that the senator's efforts had garnered ten-minute, early-morning stops in Medford (at 2:15 a.m.) and Ashland (at 3:00 a.m.).

Upon learning of the senator's success, Ashland mayor Johnson issued a front-page proclamation in the *Ashland Tidings*, urging a demonstration of "Ashland spirit." Nearly three thousand Ashlanders answered the mayor's call, but they answered it silently. Ashland's greetings differed dramatically from most; several minutes of silence were observed once the train arrived, followed by a more boisterous scene. Soon after the celebrations started, a baby was seated on the relic and Chinese fireworks were ignited. It seems that the photograph from the Southern Oregon Historical Society photo is a testimony to the excitement and patriotism that Ashland citizens shared with their countrymen over one hundred years ago, at a crucial time in America's history.

12

A New York–Style Adirondack Camp in the Middle of Ashland's Watershed?

Ashland was not upstate New York. What's this all about?
Who allowed this and why?

By August 1921, a campground, including a six-room log structure and outbuildings, had been built six miles up the canyon in Ashland's watershed. The "camp" had been constructed in the rustic style that was popular in the Adirondack Mountains of Northeastern New York, and it included a main lodge, a large barn with divided stables, a chicken house, a concrete swimming pool and guest cabins. Electricity, along with a unique shower that sprayed water from all sides, was added to the lodge in 1922. And everything was built without a septic system or sewer. So, what is the backstory? Town councils don't usually let individuals foul a town's only source of drinking water, but it seems that the town of Ashland, Oregon, needed a source of income.

Previous efforts to create a health resort like the one in Saratoga Springs, New York, had fizzled out in Oregon. But there was a vocal part of the area's business community that did not want to give up on the idea. This contingent argued that a resort would be a terrific tourist draw. However, others in the community opposed any further efforts to build the resort, as they felt that it was too expensive and impractical.

At a 1919 New York City Advertising Club meeting, former normal school professor and spokesman for the Ashland Commercial Club (forerunner to the chamber of commerce) Irving Vining talked glowingly of Ashland's

Jesse Winburn's Adirondack camp in the Ashland watershed. *Courtesy of Southern Oregon Historical Society.*

charm and its great potential to be another location for a major health spa. Avoiding any reference to the differing opinions back home, Vining made the case that town leaders were much in favor of the development. The president of the New York Advertising Club, Jesse Winburn, heard the speech and became instantly fascinated with the idea of retiring in Ashland. Raised by a large, poor Jewish family in New York City, Winburn had made a fortune with his idea of using advertising on subways and street cars. His net worth in 1920 was $1.5 million ($22 million in 2020), so why would he even think about leaving such a successful life for faraway Oregon? Professor Vining's convincing arguments about the opportunities out west and Winburn's nasty pending divorce may have influenced his decision. Winburn and his wife had already separated, and Ashland was a long way from all of the resulting emotional strife and settlement costs.

Winburn contacted Vining shortly after his speech and indicated that he wanted to visit Ashland in the beginning of 1920. After a ride through Lithia Park, up the canyon and toward Mount Ashland, Jesse Winburn set his sights on an old cabin in a meadow. Having visited several camps of wealthy New Yorkers in the Adirondack Mountains, Winburn could envision his life among all of Oregon's wilderness and beauty. He knew what he wanted, and with Vining's help, he purchased the former homestead property. An additional trip to Lithia Mineral Springs, which was about four miles

Visitors at Winburn's lodge in February 1922, apparently undaunted by the deep snow. *Photograph courtesy of Terry Skibby.*

east of Ashland, was orchestrated by community proponents of the spa resort. All that was needed to build the spa, they pointed out, was some "seed money." Two weeks in town was all it took to convince Winburn of Ashland's potential to become a kind of Saratoga of the West. Winburn thought he had found a place where he could do good work and leave his domestic problems behind. First, however, he had to return to New York and liquidate his financial holdings. Meanwhile, Vining convinced him to leave the Ashland investments in his and other community leaders' hands. During Winburn's absence, his money was used to secure options on both a hotel and the mineral springs and to buy the cabin and its surrounding 160 acres outright. These purchases made Jesse Winburn a major player in the plans to revive the notion of making Ashland a significant health resort.

On his return to Ashland, in the spring of 1921, Jesse was accompanied by two guests who also planned to become Ashland residents: syndicated humor columnist Bert Moses and his wife. When he remembered that the clearing and rustic cabin had been acquired for him in his absence, Winburn immediately took his guests there for a picnic in a chauffeur-driven limousine. This was where Jesse wanted to live and expand the old one-room log cabin into a lodge. He wanted his lodge to be a retreat for newspapermen and others in the advertising business. All was well until Winburn discovered that the property he had purchased was in the town

Jesse Winburn and friends enjoying the "good life" at his Adirondack-style camp. *Courtesy of Southern Oregon Historical Society.*

watershed. He felt cheated and lied to. What's more, Winburn stunned the local spa proponents by rejecting the options that had been made in his absence. Once again, he accused Professor Vining and attorney E.D. Briggs of lying to him and misleading him. Vining and Briggs said that they thought they had Winburn's blessing to obtain options on a hotel and mineral springs pipeline while he was in New York. As to the cabin and land in the watershed, they said that they had both convinced the town council to allow the sale because they were concerned Winburn wouldn't support the spa project if he didn't get what he wanted.

Winburn was angry and certain that he had been taken advantage of. He immediately opted out of the hotel and mineral springs options but kept the watershed property he had purchased in good faith, and he developed it as he saw fit. In all fairness to Vining and Briggs, fifteen years earlier, the Commercial Club had already developed a road that led to the cabin in the watershed to encourage tourism of Mount Ashland. At best, the town council was sending mixed signals. Did they want to close off the area—which was mostly a forested reserve—to protect the town's water supply, or did they conclude that they desperately needed Winburn's good graces and financial resources? When Jesse approached the council about improving the road to his cabin, they offered to buy him out instead.

Unwilling to sell, Winburn spent huge sums of money to expand the log structure into a lodge, with numerous outbuildings and a lighted driveway. The lodge's rustic, handmade furniture and a massive stone fireplace complemented its interior. Jesse gave his camp the name Sap and Salt in the Woods, after the newspaper column that his friend Bert Moses published from an office in downtown Ashland. Enormous parties and picnics were thrown for both adults and children at the campground. Soon, though, Winburn's swimming pool, which drained back into the creek; grazing livestock near the creek; and the cesspool for waste caught the attention of

Sap and Salt: Quips and Quotes

SAP AND SALT
ASHLAND
OREGON

Postcard return advertisement and byline for Winburn's friend Bert Moses's newspaper column "Sap and Salt" that Winburn named his lodge after. *Author's collection.*

Not much remains of the Winburn camp in the Ashland watershed, with the exception of some foundations and this sign attached to a tree. *Author's collection.*

the Ashland Board of Health. Winburn's habit of picnicking wherever he wanted and fishing in the creek also raised concerns, but he continued to do as he pleased, ignoring the numerous violation notices and simply paying the fines levied against him.

Aside from his seeming lack of care for the town's rules, Winburn was extremely generous to Ashland. He gave out prize money to the participants of the town's Fourth of July parade; he paid for completion of the Women's Civic Improvement Club building; he imported swans from Holland for Lithia Park's ponds; and he completed an overhaul of the town's hospital at a cost of $500,000 in today's money—all during a two-year period. Yet, Jesse felt more and more as though he was underappreciated by the town (even though it named a street through Lithia Park in his honor). He felt that he was always being asked to fund something else and that he was continually accused of fouling the water supply, so he decided to sell out and end his stay.

By some accounts, the City of Ashland acquired the property from Winburn in the summer of 1923, promptly sold its contents and secured a gate across the road to the cabin, blocking unauthorized access. However, a different version of the story reported that Winburn returned from a worldwide trip in 1925 and briefly stayed with Bert Moses and his wife at Sap and Salt. A month later, in August 1925, Ashland's local paper reported the sale of the property to the City of Ashland. A third account, which has been attributed to Winburn's chauffeur, indicated that after advertising the sale of the lodge in statewide newspapers, Winburn received no offers and simply gave the property to the city.

Regardless of the timing and process of the sale, the town of Ashland was finally able to end Winburn's tenure in the watershed and protect the city's water supply. Over time, the buildings deteriorated and became hazardous, forcing the Forest Service and the city to tear them down in the early 1960s. Today, only the concrete walkways and Winburn's eight-foot-deep swimming pool remain on the property.

13

NOT YOUR GRANDFATHER'S KKK

Jokingly referred to as the "Peoples' Republic of Ashland" for its liberal reputation, how does one explain the town's robust historical flirtation with the Klan?

Great confusion exists in America regarding the Ku Klux Klan (KKK) and its history. Most of that confusion comes from the way textbooks and instructors present the topic in schools, as well as how the Klan has been portrayed in the popular culture. Most Americans know two versions of the Klan—both are racist, violent and located in the Southern states. One version of the Klan was founded at the end of the Civil War and is often referenced in history texts and accounts of the Reconstruction era. The KKK of the 1950s and 1960s existed to maintain Jim Crow laws and segregation and to oppose civil rights advocates. Many Americans saw the Klan's heritage of violence and racial hatred displayed live in their living rooms on television and later in movies and television documentaries. With these versions of the Klan in mind, it is difficult to visualize three hundred Klansmen in full regalia parading down Ashland's Main Street and the plaza as they did in the early 1920s.

A September 1924 town event included the appearance of an airplane, with an electrically illuminated cross circling above. At the same time a huge cross burned on a nearby hillside. This appearance was followed by a naturalization ceremony and the initiation of nine new local Klan members; ice cream was served by the Ladies of the Invisible Empire at a local lodge. Was this some kind aberration in a town where Chautauqua flourished and

A campaign sign for the 2008 election, signifying total support for the Democratic candidate. *Author's collection.*

residents fought to bring back their small college from state budget cuts and rallied to open a Carnegie library? No, it wasn't—not really.

The Ku Klux Klan of the 1910s and early 1920s, which appears in numerous photographs from Ashland, was different from the Klan that most Americans are familiar with, and it is often ignored in texts and media— or, at best, treated as a short-lived phenomenon. Ironically, the Klan of the 1920s was far more wide-spread and popular, and it was not limited to the South. So, what was the difference between this version and the traditional version of the Klan? What was its appeal, and why did it find sympathy in a town that was mostly made up of white Protestants who favored Prohibition? As the Ashland Commercial Club's (forerunner to the chamber of commerce) promotional pamphlet stated in 1915, the town population was "almost wholly American, no negroes or Japanese."

The KKK of the 1920s was engaged in a serious attempt to rebrand and spread nationwide. Klansmen did not want to think of themselves as racists and religious bigots, as the previous iteration had been labeled; instead, they wanted to view themselves as patriots who were safeguarding America and their hometowns from a very real foreign threat. The Klan's appeal to morality and patriotism transcended normal Republican and Democratic Party politics. For thirty years, the United States had a large influx of immigrants from eastern and southern Europe, and many of these immigrants were non-Protestants. The common literature of the period warned that these newcomers had pledged their allegiances to a foreign power. The early twentieth century was a time when calls to restrict a particular religion could be voiced openly, even unapologetically. This was partly because the recent World War had created strong anti-foreign feelings in the United States; by extension, it was not difficult for Protestant Americans to see Catholicism and Judaism as "foreign religions." Many feared that the United States would "go Catholic by immigration."

Opposed to all violations of Prohibition, the citizens of Ashland had a long history of keeping their town dry. In this regard, the pursuit of bootleggers was just as monitored by the particularly influential local Woman's Christian Temperance Union as the town's law enforcement. To

Early 1920s Ku Klux Klan march in downtown Ashland. *Author's collection.*

many in Ashland, the Klan of that time had a valid position to uphold the law and morality of the land; Klan membership applications even included a temperance pledge. This "respect for the law" and dedication to the end of lawlessness strongly appealed to Ashland's general population. It was an effective part of the Klan's efforts to change its image and, thereby, appear more mainstream. What's more, urban Catholics and Jews were often linked to efforts to end Prohibition and were consequently seen as individuals who encouraged drinking and the breakdown of morality. Many in the town feared that Ashland's rural Protestant dominance of traditional American values was ending.

Unlike the southern Klan, which most Americans learned about in school, the 1920s KKK groomed its public persona and stressed its nonviolent nature and progressive legislative goals. The 1922 Oregon School Bill was the Klan's most successful legislative effort. Scottish Rite Masons actually introduced the proposed legislation, and the Klan was quick to promote it as a very American, nonelitist law. Although similar bills were introduced in other states, Oregon's was the only successful measure. The bill made a public-school education required for any child between the ages of eight and sixteen; this, the Klan maintained, showed its benevolent concern for the education of children. It was free, public education, after all, that made America's "melting pot" work. Besides, as one Jackson County parent opined, "What is good enough for my children is good enough for anybody's children." A one-hundred-dollar-per-day fine was to be levied against noncomplying parents.

The Klan's real goal for the compulsory school law was to block the existence of Catholic schools. Jacksonville had the only parochial school in southern Oregon at the time. Public schools held the promise of American unity by teaching a common history, language and value system. Requiring young people to get such an education certainly sounded like a worthy effort, and the proposed law got a large majority vote in Ashland. However, by 1925, both the Oregon and U.S. Supreme Courts had declared the legislative act unconstitutional, and the law was never implemented. Other Klan initiatives that appealed to mainstream citizens included support for improved state roads and greater funding for public education.

Most Ashlanders did not formally join the Klan, and the vast majority of those who did tended to be ordinary citizens. Former Ashland Klansmen often explained that, to them, the organization seemed to be more of a fraternal club than a terrorist group. The local Klan held picnics, helped some unfortunate citizens with food and clothing and conducted citizenship ceremonies. These activities legitimized the KKK in the eyes of many by making it look like any other fraternal group. Some in Ashland, which was a mostly dry town overwhelmingly made up of white, native-born Christians, found the cleverly rebranded Klan's messages appealing, as they felt that their rural values were increasingly questioned, and their country was changing. In the early 1920s, a Ku Klux Klan chapter in Ashland was not as much of an aberration as it may appear to be. In fact, one could argue that it would have been odd if 1920s Ashland, with its demographic and political profile, had not joined the forty-nine other Oregon towns and cities with Klan chapters.

14

Why Are the Ashes of a Famous Novelist and the Grave of a Legendary Country Singer in a Remote Ashland Cemetery?

Both Erskine Caldwell and Rose Maddox are interred just across the Interstate 5 freeway, in Scenic Hills Memorial Park, about as far away from their southern roots as they could possibly end up. Caldwell was born in 1903 in White Oak, Georgia, although Moreland, Georgia, is the site of a museum in his honor. At her birth, in 1925, Rose Maddox joined a family of six other children in Boaz, Alabama. An ironic common denominator of Caldwell and Maddox—in addition to their final resting place—was their firsthand knowledge of the hopelessly poor and degrading lives of sharecroppers in the 1930s in the Deep South, and they both used their own unique skills to portray them. While Erskine later wrote novels about the rural poor, whose lives he had witnessed while traveling between churches in central Georgia with his minister father, Rose wrote and sang songs about the tenant-sharecropper life she was born into in Alabama.

Caldwell's publications of *Tobacco Road* (1932) and *God's Little Acre* (1933) made him both famous and infamous. He went on to write more than fifty books, selling over 80 million copies worldwide before his death at the age of eighty-three. Fellow southern author William Faulkner praised him as one the best American writers of his time, alongside Thomas Wolfe and Ernest Hemingway. Caldwell's style of writing, though, was not, initially, universally approved. His depictions of Depression-era, rural, poor southerners were considered obscene by many, and they even resulted in his arrest at a New

York book signing for *God's Little Acre*. In several cities, his books were banned and seized. Defending his work, Caldwell always maintained that he was not a crusader trying to change the world but an observer, telling a story by reporting about the people he knew growing up. He had lived in the same neighborhoods and had gone to the same schools as the poor tenant farmers, and he witnessed their dialect, behavior and attitudes that were later reflected in his novels. Until adulthood, he maintained that he didn't know much about life outside of the South.

Over time, the bans on Caldwell's books were lifted, and his books were returned to library shelves. Both of his best-known titles were eventually made into Hollywood movies. An adaptation of *Tobacco Road* even played on Broadway for over seven years, resulting in Caldwell receiving royalty checks for thousands of dollars during the height of the Great Depression in the 1930s. Eventually, he was even invited back to Georgia for open houses, lectures and Sunday picnics that honored him and his work. An Erskine Caldwell Museum, complete with the relocated house he was born in, can still be found in the town square of Moreland, Georgia.

Caldwell traveled widely, divorced three wives and married four times. It was his fourth wife, Virginia Fletcher, who was also the illustrator of two of his later travel books, who brought his ashes to Ashland, Oregon. In the early 1970s, when Caldwell's stepson, Drew Fletcher, indicated an interest in moving up the coast, from Los Angeles, to become a full-time writer himself, Erskine urged him to look seriously at the scenic college town of Ashland. He remembered it fondly from a nationwide lecture tour, during which he had spoken at Southern Oregon College (Southern Oregon University today). On a scouting trip for a new location, Drew and his wife fell in love with Ashland and moved north in 1975.

Annually, the Caldwells would visit Drew and his family while staying at the Ashland Hills Inn. At one point, they even considered moving to Ashland themselves, but Erskine wanted to be near an airport with more direct flights, so they remained in Arizona until his death in 1987. In a desire to be close to her remaining family, Virginia moved to Medford, Oregon's Rogue Valley Manor, a retirement center about twelve miles from Ashland. Despite the fact that Erskine Caldwell never lived in Ashland, and only knew it as a visitor, Drew and his mother, Virginia, felt that it was appropriate for him to be interred near his family of thirty years. While residing in Ashland, Drew had befriended the owners of the Scenic Hills Memorial Cemetery, and upon seeing it, thought it would be a quiet, secure and beautiful resting place for his famous stepfather.

Erskine Caldwell's ashes are located in an Ashland, Oregon cemetery, even though he never lived there. *Author's collection.*

On the other hand, Rose Maddox—often referred to as "the sweetheart of hillbilly swing"—*did* live in Ashland during the latter part of her five-decade career. As Ken Burn's 2020 PBS film series, *Country Music*, pointed out, the Maddox Brothers and Rose had already established themselves as "the most colorful hillbilly band in America" by the time they came to Ashland. Their flamboyant, Hollywood-tailored western costumes and raucous stage antics caused them to stand out in a crowded field. Yet not unlike many of the country performers Rose would work with (including Johnny Cash, Merle Haggard, Buck Owens and Bill Monroe), her climb from Alabama sharecropper and California "fruit tramp" to fame was hardly assured. In fact, the only reason Rose was even initially included in her brothers' band was because the radio station where the band got its start would only put them on the air if they had a female singer. So, her brothers quickly added eleven-year-old Rose to their band.

It was Lula Maddox, Rose's mother, who decided the family needed to leave their tenant farm and join the exodus to the "promised land" of California (à la Steinbeck's *Grapes of Wrath*). After selling all of their family possessions for thirty-five dollars, Lula; her husband, Charlie; and their five unmarried children "rode the rails" to Oakland, California. While working as migrant farm laborers in California's agricultural areas, the

Right: "The Maddox Brothers and Rose," as they appeared in their prime. *Author's collection.*

Below: The Maddox Ranch just east of Interstate 5 and visible from the freeway. *Author's collection.*

boys soon tired of the backbreaking work they did for little pay. The whole family could play musical instruments, and they saw music as a way out of this drudgery. The band, especially Rose, became immensely successful in the country music world by the late 1930s and postwar 1940s. Weekly radio shows, record album recordings, appearances at the Grand Ole Opry and Louisiana Hayride and countless one-night performances all contributed to their success.

After piling into the fleet of Cadillacs they toured in, the band would stop and play on an Ashland radio station (KCMX) every summer. Rose's brother Don said the Ashland area had spectacular beauty and that he planned to

The grave of famous country singer Rose Maddox in Scenic Hills Memorial Park Cemetery. *Author's collection.*

someday buy a ranch there. In 1958, he did just that. Don purchased three hundred acres for $27,500; the land was just east of town, and he raised cattle there. Shortly thereafter, Rose and the remaining family members joined him on a five-acre section of the property, and once again they performed locally and throughout the Northwest. The band's local venues included the Ashland Elks Lodge, Talent City Hall, Medford's 21 Club and Lindy's in Roseburg. In a 1992 interview, Rose said she particularly remembered performances in Roseburg because of the fistfights that started when the timber workers came in. She explained that the band would just keep playing when the fights started because they needed to keep everybody dancing in order to avoid a complete brawl.

Despite several heart attacks and lengthy hospitalizations, Rose miraculously continued to entertain well into the 1980s. She performed at several national folk festivals throughout the United States and Europe, and she was nominated for a Grammy Award for her album that was aptly titled *$35 and a Dream*. Today, the queen of rockabilly music, who some credit with ushering in the era of rock-and-roll, is buried within sight of the mausoleum that holds the ashes of her fellow famous ex-southerner, Caldwell.

PART VI

THE SPORTING LIFE

15

"Real Men" Played Baseball Without Gloves

It was once seen as unmanly to use anything but one's barehands to catch a ball. Ashland's undefeated town team of the 1880s played without gloves, but that's not why they were so good.

Early baseball was markedly different from the game that's played today. Gloves to help catch balls were gradually and begrudgingly adopted, and balls were pitched underhand until the mid-1880s; batters were even allowed to call the pitch to be thrown high, between the waist and shoulders, or low, between the knees and waist. Eventually, however, as pitchers began throwing overhand, catchers began wearing masks adapted from the sport of fencing, and players started wearing padded gloves, giving in to the pain of catching barehanded and making them subjects of ridicule for sissifying the sport. But none of this explains how no one could defeat Ashland's early town baseball team. Other town teams played with the same limitations, but no one would even bet against the Ashland nine.

Maybe a baseball that curved away from the batter was some sort of optical illusion. A decidedly partisan Yreka, California crowd couldn't believe what it was witnessing—it just couldn't be done. Nobody was that good. How could a new pitcher from Ashland named McConnell throw a baseball that curved horizontally? Much earlier, in June 1884, George McConnell and his Ashland teammates had climbed aboard a six-horse stagecoach headed for Yreka, California—it would be three more years before a railroad route was completed over the mountain pass, providing a much faster and comfortable

Left: Professional baseball player Billy Sunday demonstrating how he prepares to catch a baseball barehanded. *Author's collection.*

Below: A facsimile of the first style of baseball gloves, which were introduced in the late 1880s. *Author's collection.*

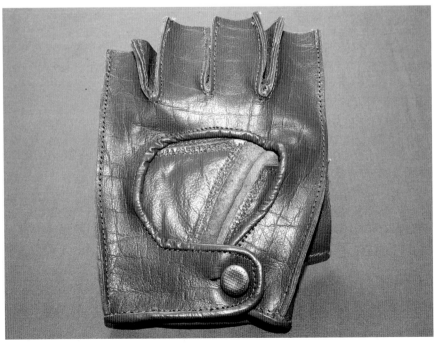

way to travel. While McConnell and his catcher, John Norris, were new to town, the rest of Ashland's team was well-stocked with pioneer family names, including Butler, Wagner, Wimer, Alford and Sears—even the umpire was a Tolman. What a day it would prove to be—ten miles from town, a brass band met the stagecoach, and a dance was planned for that evening after the lopsided 28 to 6 Ashland victory. As for Yreka fans, they were thrilled seeing the first "curved ball" ever thrown, as far as they knew.

Although the *Ashland Tidings* credited McConnell with being the first pitcher to successfully throw a curveball, an East Coast player of the 1870s is generally recognized as the first curveball pitcher. Five-foot-six Candy Cummings claimed he invented the pitch after seeing a spinning clamshell curve across the water as it was being skipped. From 1872 to 1875, Cummings won 124 games with his curveball pitch, which no one at the time knew how to hit. He threw with an underhand—but closer to sidearm—pitch, causing balls to break dramatically. But in 1884 Yreka, nobody was talking about Cummings and his clamshells—it was this McConnell fellow who fascinated them. After the game, some of Yreka's business boosters urged the Ashland ace to demonstrate how he did it. McConnell obliged by ordering that three poles be set in a line, and he then proceeded to entertain the crowd with a throwing exhibition, which was described in the June 13, 1884 edition of *Ashland Tidings*. McConnell stood to the left of the first pole and threw the ball so that it would pass to the left of the first pole, to the right of the middle one and to the left of the third pole. He then threw to make a ball curve the other way, which seemed to satisfy the gathered audience that there was no illusion involved—just considerable skill. McConnell was likely throwing both a curveball and what later would be called a screwball.

Armed with McConnell, the cocky Ashland team enjoyed numerous victories and even challenged any team that dared to $1,000 and $2,000 ($25,000 and $50,000 in 2020 dollars) matches for each of the next several seasons. There were no takers. During this period, George married into the pioneer Gillette family and soon had a small family of his own to support. Commenting on the 1888 birth of his daughter, McConnell confessed to an *Ashland Tidings* reporter that he was sorry, only because he would "not be able to make a baseball pitcher out of the new arrival." Obviously, McConnell did not anticipate the future traveling Bloomer Girls baseball teams, like the one that visited Ashland a dozen years later.

Ashland's early baseball team, "the team that made Ashland famous," remained legendary. Fifty years later, George McConnell and two of his former teammates, Gwin Butler and John Norris, made a nostalgic

NATIONAL BASEBALL HALL OF FAME & MUSEUM®
Cooperstown, New York

Above: W.A. "Candy" Cummings is generally acknowledged by the Baseball Hall of Fame as the first baseball pitcher to develop and throw a curve ball. *Author's collection.*

Right: Ashland's curveball pitcher, George McConnell, who dominated local teams. *Author's collection.*

anniversary visit to the Yreka diamond in June 1934, but this time they traveled in the relative comfort of Domingo Perozzi's automobile. While they were not greeted by a brass band, the now-aged boys of summer had not been forgotten. They found a number of Yrekans who recalled the day they saw their first "curved ball."

It appears that life after baseball continued to be rewarding for several of the Ashland nine. At the fiftieth anniversary date of their conquest over Yreka, seven of the nine were still living, with four still residing in Ashland. One of the most prominent members of the remaining seven included first baseman Gwin Butler, who went on to become Ashland's mayor in 1906; he was a very successful real estate investor and a generous donor to the needy, setting up a trust that continues to this day. Pitcher McConnell went on to run a grocery store; was elected captain of the Oregon National Guard in 1889, a year after retiring from baseball; and he became a breeder of fancy show pigeons. Second baseman M.L. Alford married Rachel Lindsey Applegate and became a Medford city recorder for twenty-seven years.

16

Hey Dad, There's a Cemetery on the Fourth Hole!

Sent to do the dirty work of cleaning up the corner of Ashland's golf course, where Highway 66 and Crowson Road meet, teenager Mike Dawkins and his tractor uncovered long-forgotten gravestones that had been obscured by brush and brambles.

Giles and Martha Wells had been dead and buried for more than thirty years when W.J. Wade of Portland began constructing Ashland's Oak Knoll Golf Course on what had once been the Wells Family Ranch in 1926. Originally designed by San Francisco Bay–area PGA golfer Sam Whiting, the nine-hole course was opened to much fanfare on June 22, 1927. Despite the course's lack of a clubhouse on opening day, enthusiasts partook in basket picnics, golf shot contests and a tournament that was organized by members of the town's recently formed golf club. Located in the Elks building, McGee's Dry Goods Store offered women the latest in golf attire, and two recent University of California graduates announced that they were going to open a golf shop, with a complete line of golfing goods, in the Ashland hotel building. The town's enthusiasm seemed to be contagious.

Despite the relatively lengthy existence of the Ashland Golf Club, the Wells family settled on the land in 1853, nearly seventy-five years before the course was built and several years before Oregon became a state. As part of a large wagon train that followed the Applegate Trail across the Green Springs, the family was warmly welcomed by the Isaac Hill family at

The Wells family gravestones uncovered at Ashland's Oak Knoll Golf Course. *Author's collection.*

The newly completed Oak Knoll Golf Course as it looked in 1927. Today, this is the third hole green. *Oak Knoll Golf Course collection.*

their cabin, which was located where Emigrant Lake is today. The Hills had recently taken refuge with other settlers in a stockade at Wagner Creek to protect themselves from a three-year war with the local Native Americans. A wagon train of newcomers was, for the Hill family, a most encouraging sight.

With the forced removal of native people to reservations up north, Giles, Martha Wells and their eight children took advantage of a donation land claim and settled on several hundred acres of land that included the future site of the Ashland golf course. There, Giles built a sawmill and blacksmith shop on Tolman Creek and a stately white frame house that still stands across the highway from the entrance to Oak Knoll Golf Course. The Wellses were prominent early pioneers in the area where they settled, which was a couple of miles southeast of the village that was then called Ashland Mills. They had been married and lived in several other states long before their move to Oregon. Giles, like so many men of his era, had taken part in the 1849 California gold rush. After the couple's arrival in the Ashland area, Giles raised and led a company of volunteers during the Rogue Indian Wars. He also served a term in the Oregon legislature as a representative from Jackson County. Both Giles and Martha had lived long lives and passed away within a few months of each other; Giles died in December 1894, at the age of ninety-five, and Martha died in September 1894, at the age of eighty-eight.

On a Tuesday evening in February 1926, in the newly built Lithia Springs Hotel, Rogue Valley boosters met to discuss the construction of a golf club in Ashland. The session was organized by a small group of concerned downtown Ashland businessmen who had become convinced that the town needed a golf course. The reports from the automobile registration office in Lithia Park were disturbing; when the session was informed that numerous "auto tourists" were not interested in staying in a town without a course— and that they would skip Ashland for a town with a golf course—they knew business would suffer. For several years, the Lithia Auto Camp had been significant in getting travelers to stay in Ashland for a few extra days and spend their disposable income in local businesses.

Those who attended the 1926 golf club organizational meeting quickly settled on a construction site east of town, which was identified as the "Elliott tract." Over the years, the Wells family had sold off pieces of their land claim to others. This particular piece of property had the added advantage of facing the Pacific Highway (Highway 66), which many thought would increase business interest in the area, and the group felt that the site's connection to the Talent Irrigation District (TID) would also provide more than enough water. The group planned to hold a follow-up meeting after a significant membership drive was conducted; the goal of the drive was to gain one hundred members.

While the site had ample room for nine holes, even today, golfers who tend to "slice" their tee shots on the existing par-three fourth hole sometimes find their balls landing near the resting places of Giles, Martha and two of their children. The family traditionally buried their dead on a long-forgotten corner of their land, which was a common custom in earlier times. Long hidden and mostly forgotten, the Wells cemetery was discovered by young Mike Dawkins after his father leased the course from the city in the early 1960s.

Historically, golf courses seem to be particularly impacted by the ebb and flow of both the national and regional economy and Ashland's course is no exception. Even the prestigious, nearby Rogue Valley Country Club had its fair share of stops and starts until later in the 1920s, when twenty-eight new courses were simultaneously opened throughout Oregon. Hard times followed, with the Great Depression of the 1930s and, later, World War II. Many courses closed and never reopened, but Ashland's Oak Knoll Golf Course limped through the 1930s. The *Ashland Tidings* editor even urged locals to support the golf course as part of their civic duty. In his "The Editor's Last Word" column, he preached the virtues of fresh air, companionship and healthy recreation. He even argued that, after Lithia Park, the course was Ashland's second-greatest attraction. However, like so many courses in Oregon, the nine-hole course was closed during World War II, not to be reopened until the 1950s, when it was identified as "Ashland's new golf course" in a chamber of commerce brochure. By 1961, yet another promotional brochure listed the Oak Knoll Golf Café as a restaurant that specialized in steak dinners, and nine holes of golf could be played for $1.00 on weekdays. Cart rentals and weekend rounds increased the price of play to $2.00.

From the course's beginnings, in 1926 and 1927, it was always anticipated that it would expand from nine to eighteen holes, but a serious proposal didn't take shape until the mid-1960s. The course's additional nine holes were part of a development called the "Oak Knoll Project," which was put forth by Mike's father Bill Hawkins and his partner, Jack Reid. Hawkins had been impressed by the success of the Rogue Valley Manor, a retirement facility with a golf course in Medford, so he decided to take over the lease of the Oak Knoll Golf Course from the city and its previous operator and began building an adjoining residential community, which was initially restricted to buyers without children. Before long, the concept morphed into

A 1950s Oak Knoll Golf Course advertising matchbook. *Author's collection.*

a full eighteen-hole, multifaceted proposal that was open to all families and levels of golfers.

As presented, city officials, an adjoining land owner, a complex financing plan and the two major developers all needed to work diligently to keep the ambitious notion alive. The proposal included acquiring an additional sixty acres to expand the course, which would be renamed Green Springs Country Club. A new clubhouse, with locker rooms and a sauna bath, along with the retention of the existing structure, an Olympic-sized swimming pool, a 100-unit motel and a convention center complex with seating for 250 were all part of the plan. The funds for the course would be raised through tax exempt revenue bonds and a 1 percent increase in the town's hotel-motel tax.

Oak Knoll remains a nine-hole course, without the amenities proposed. For a variety of reasons, Dawkins's and other subsequent proposals haven't taken shape; perhaps they have all been overly ambitious with flawed financial plans. Nevertheless, the family-friendly homes within the adjoining subdivision have mushroomed into a sizable community, and it remains best to avoid a tee shot too far to the right of the fourth hole, where the Wells family remains at rest.

PART VII
BRINGING THEM IN

17

SHAKESPEARE BEFORE BOWMER

Twenty-seven years before the Oregon Shakespeare Festival began, one could see Shakespeare performed by a professional theater company in downtown Ashland.

The story of Ashland's first Shakespearean festival in 1935 boarders on myth. Angus Bowmer's experiment of filling an old Chautauqua shell with Shakespearean plays, complete with a green show of afternoon boxing matches is legendary. But what about Charles B. Hanford, the first to perform Shakespeare professionally in Ashland—and for a three-year run?

A full quarter century before Angus Bowmer played Shylock, Charles Hanford brought a cast of thirty to Ashland's opera house to perform *Merchant of Venice.* Hanford had been performing in Shakespearean plays for twenty years when he first appeared in Ashland in 1908. He had previously played Marc Antony opposite the leading actor of his time, Edwin Booth— the brother of John Wilkes Booth—in the 1880s. Interestingly, the only time the Booth brothers acted together, John Wilkes played Marc Antony. Hanford, Ashland's future Shakespearean performer, took the place of a presidential assassin.

Touring actors were commonplace in nineteenth century America and varied greatly in quality. Mark Twain poked fun at much of the lower end of the spectrum with his portrayal of the Duke and King in *The Adventures of Huckleberry Finn.* Charles Hanford, on the other hand, was listed in *Who Was Who in America*, as well as in a listing of significant actors at the turn of

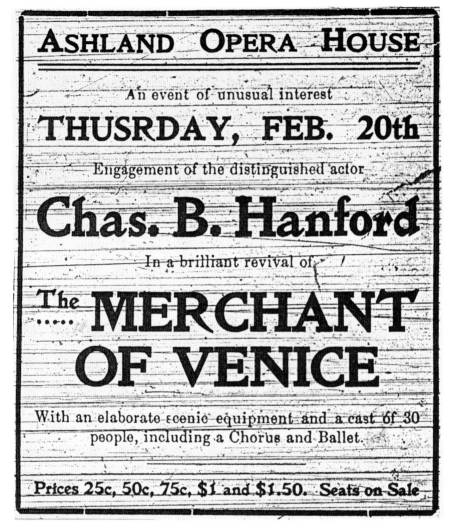

Ashland newspaper advertisement for Hanford's Shakespeare company presentation. *Courtesy of* Ashland Tidings.

the century. In addition to the prominent Edwin Booth, Hanford worked and toured with some of the best-known actors and actresses of his time, including Louis James, John E. Kellerd and Kathryn Kidder. Seven years before his first Ashland appearance, Hanford had already been profiled in *Players of the Present*, a series of biographical sketches of prominent American stage actors. Born in California and raised in Washington, D.C., Charles Hanford had studied law at Columbia University but soon turned to the stage, as he found acting to be a more compatible profession. After playing numerous Shakespearean roles on tours with a variety of companies, Hanford struck out on his own in 1898, when he headed a Shakespearean revival company. It was in this position that he came to Ashland's opera house each February for three straight years.

Well-advertised with pictures, display advertisements, prepared newspaper copy and even an advance man, the Charles Hanford Company first descended on Ashland as part of its West Coast tour in February 1908. Only Ashland had the chance to see *The Merchant of Venice* performed between the towns of Chico, California, and Eugene, Oregon. This wasn't totally by chance, as Ashland had a suitable downtown opera house, direct passenger train access and a reputation for hosting Chautauqua each summer for fifteen years.

Judging from the phrasing of the profuse praise for Hanford's talents, it appears the *Ashland Tidings* printed the company's advance press releases verbatim. Three days before Hanford's performance, the local paper reported, "Mr. Hanford enjoys a following such as few players can boast. He has the faculty of making every part he plays distinctly human, which fascinates the senses and delights the intelligence." Advertisements, complete with the enticement of an elaborate set and a large cast that included a chorus and ballet, ran throughout February, announcing the coming event. Two pictures were printed in the town's newspapers: one with Hanford as Shylock in an enormous, flowing beard, and one of him without a costume that had been taken earlier in the month.

After Hanford's one-night performance, the *Tidings* review was all praise, if a little reserved. "Taken as a whole, the entertainment was one of the most successful events in dramatic circles in the city." A large and, reportedly, enthusiastic audience greeted the production, and Hanford was praised for his portrayal of Shylock. The review concluded with the stated hope that Hanford's company would return, especially because Ashland had provided such a warm reception. And return he did. The next two years would see Hanford's Shakespearean road show arriving in Ashland each February.

Much Ado About Nothing was the company's 1909 offering, and, as usual, newspaper advertisements, press releases and an advance man were used to ensure that the company was greeted by a full house and smooth operations. But it was not to be. It seems that the company's baggage, which contained the costumes and props, did not arrive in time for the Friday evening event. Unable to perform the Shakespearean comedy, Hanford entertained the packed house with vaudeville routines and old stories of his experiences with Edwin Booth and other famous actors. Finally, the trunks arrived, and Hanford ended his stall. The original play was performed, causing the entire program to last until 1:30 a.m. The *Tidings* reviewer praised the Hanford Company production and indicated that his assumption was that "probably the ninety and nine people out of any given hundred would regard the reading of Shakespeare as dry matter," but, under the direction of Hanford and Company, it was a revelation. Because of the delay and consequential late conclusion, the local opera house manager apologized profusely and explained that if any other traveling company would have been involved, he would have canceled the planned performance—but this was Charles Hanford.

Returning for yet another February performance in 1910, Hanford was not forced to use his considerable ad lib talents, as the cast and luggage all arrived at the opera house simultaneously. The play was billed as "the event of the season," which the *Tidings* admitted was a "trite prediction"; but, by then, Hanford's reputation in Ashland was secure enough to make the claim. The Friday performance of *The Taming of the Shrew* was, as usual, a sellout. The *Tidings* reviewer waxed, "Hanford is always a welcome visitor here, and his appearance is looked forward to with pleasure, as affording an exhibition of the legitimate drama faithfully and skillfully presented." Praise went both ways, as Hanford's advance man, Lawrence Walker, complimented the town on its start toward new paved streets, which had occurred since his previous visit.

However, Walker was not able to see those streets completed, as Hanford's Shakespearean tours were numbered. By 1911, Hanford was off the circuit and acting in New York. He starred in a number of plays until 1917, when, at the age of fifty-eight, he enlisted in the navy, where his path would cross with still another historical American figure. After being assigned to the office of navy intelligence, Hanford worked under the direction of Thomas Alva Edison, who is best known for the invention of the phonograph and incandescent lamp. Edison and his team of workers contributed forty-five inventions during the war, including defensive instruments that were used against German U-boats. After World War I, Hanford stayed on as a writer for the naval research lab that was established by Edison. But by 1926, Charles Hanford's eventful life would come to an end.

Clearly, Angus Bowmer and Shakespeare in Ashland are forever tied together, and rightfully so. Yet the bold idea of bringing professional Shakespearean actors to a rural town in southern Oregon actually happened long before Angus Bowmer got the inspiration. An equally adventuresome lover of Shakespeare, Charles Hanford preceded him on the stage in Ashland.

18

Auto Campers of the Past Were Welcomed Guests in Lithia Park. Not So Today.

No person shall camp within the park limits within the City of Ashland…
—Ashland Municipal Code 10.68.330

Freed from train schedules and marginal inner-city hotels, middle-class auto campers set out for adventures to enjoy the innocence of early motoring. The transition from wagons to cars was liberating and created a whole new form of recreation. With the advent of automobile travel, nightfall just meant pulling over into a farmer's field and camping under the stars until morning. It was not long, however, before angry farmers resented the use of their land for someone else's recreation and began chasing auto campers away. Meanwhile, small-town merchants saw a new potential market for their goods; they just needed to lure motorists to their town to stay awhile. Free municipal auto camps seemed to provide the answer.

Towns competed for the business of camping motorists; they offered everything, from electric lights and hot water, to free firewood and, usually, a central facility with showers and a kitchen. Later, tent sites were replaced by small, two-hundred-square-foot cabins that provided a number of comforts, such as indoor plumbing, a good bed and, likely, a greater sense of personal security. Over time, competition led to an increased refinement of these campgrounds.

Ashland formally opened its own auto camp on July 22, 1915. With all of the well-off tourists who were traveling to and from San Francisco for the Pan-American Exposition of 1915, the Ashland business community was all

109

for hosting some of these folks who were engaged in motor touring. This early establishment of Ashland's auto camp may explain why a 1925 *Oregonian* staff writer credited Ashland with "having the undisputed distinction of being first in the United States." However, the claim has only had partial collaboration and is disputed by another nearby southern Oregon town, Grants Pass. For years, attendees who descended on Ashland's Chautauqua had filled Lithia Park with automobiles for two weeks each summer, so the early claim may have validity. Whatever the case, the expanded concept of a dedicated, year-round auto camp seemed attractive. But Ashland's citizens were initially equally divided into "enthusiasts" and those who deemed an auto camp in Lithia Park as a "fool's notion." The skeptics were referred to as "knockers." In a very short time, though, even "knockers" came to see the advantage of year-round tourism.

From the beginning, the Lithia Park camp was rated as superior to most. It featured the health-giving Lithia spring water, a magnificent wooded natural setting, an unlimited length of stay, an opportunity to cook with gas and, for the first seven years, it was all free. With rave reviews, especially from California auto tourists, the campground's reputation of being a clean, cheerful and safe place to enjoy was enhanced. A California writer even praised the camp for being the finest auto park on the West Coast; he maintained that the cabins were unusually clean and came complete with landscaping, including flowers and shrubs—he likened them to a small home. Continuous improvements and upgrades, however, eventually required the campground to acquire a local $10,000 bond and enforce a daily charge of fifty cents per car, beginning in the 1923 season. Furthermore, there seemed to be an undercurrent of concern that the "free admission" had been attracting, what some citizens referred to as, "riff-raff," or "undesirables," who might have driven away "good spenders." Despite this concern, the campground's number of auto tourists throughout the 1920s and early 1930s was staggering for a town with six thousand permanent residents—during some years, as many as ten thousand campers were registered. The auto camp's attendance became a kind of barometer for the local business community.

According to advertising from this period, by 1930, Ashland had added twenty new cabins to the campground's existing twenty for a one-time total of "forty modern cabins" to accommodate the steady demand. The new cabins featured two rooms, gas cooking fixtures, showers and toilets, two beds, tables, sinks with washbasins, wardrobes closets and curtains—there was even a laundry wagon that picked up wash daily. The campground had

Above: Grand opening of Ashland's auto camp in Lithia Park. *Courtesy of Southern Oregon Historical Society.*

Right: Eventually, Ashland's Lithia Auto Camp had to charge for stays using a punch-card system. *Author's collection.*

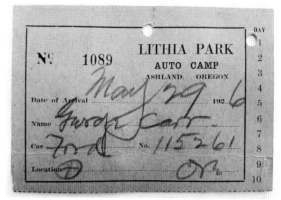

become one of the first "Auto Camps DE lux" to be written about nationally. Yet none of this could protect Ashland from the economic forces that were far beyond its ability to control.

In the mid-1930s, privately run auto courts or "motels" began to dot the nation's roads and highways, capturing traffic from the city-operated auto camps that were usually located in town parks off the road. This, coupled with a nationwide depression and a World War, shifted local business owners' concerns, as municipal-owned and maintained tourist camps became much lower city priorities. Eventually, most were leased to private individuals or simply neglected. By the 1950s, the Ashland Park Commission decided to notify the current lease holder that the auto camp was to be phased out. It was just not economically responsible for the city to maintain the deteriorating cabins that were in need of a complete rebuilding. In 1961, the cabins were demolished, leaving only the recreation and registration building and a single cabin next door, which was used for years to store the town's Christmas decorations. Today, the large lighted sign that was once located on the plaza and directed auto tourists to the registration office, as well as the park store and gas filling station, is missing. The recreation and registration building is still used by the park department, and the adjoining single cabin has been restored in a joint effort by the parks department and the Southern Oregon Historical Society as a reminder of what once was.

For a time in the 1960s, the recreation and registration building was leased out as a natural history museum, and a small zoo existed nearby. However, all traces of the once sprawling auto campground were gone by the mid-1960s, and perhaps the once welcoming attitudes left with them. A new influx of campers, who displayed behaviors that distressed many locals, descended on the park. According to longtime park board commissioner and local businessman Charles Scripter, the park was overrun with "a young irresponsible generation and their dogs, alienating the very generation whose property taxes pay for maintenance and beautification of the park."

The last-remaining restored Lithia Auto Camp cabin on the old campgrounds. *Photograph courtesy of Terry Skibby.*

In his 1975 brief history of the park, Scripter went on to state that "'long-hairs' and 'hippies' used the park for all purposes, including a living area by day and night." Additionally, he said, "We never know which bush hides an exhibitionist and what pot party we will interrupt, so we keep our children home and do not picnic in the park." Scripter was likely reflecting the views of many in Ashland, especially the business community, who often found that these new campers were more of a nuisance than an economic benefit.

Currently, no overnight camping is allowed in Lithia Park—a dramatic departure from the days of Chautauqua and tourist motoring. Some may wish to attach a kind of Marxian interpretation to this historical change, vilifying the citizens for being welcoming only when their economic advantage is in play. However, others maintain that it is simply a logical reflection of the changing times and an example of how overt behaviors can impact and affect attitudes.

19

FDR's New Deal and a Fledgling Shakespeare Festival

Ashland's famous award-winning Shakespeare festival had its beginnings in the middle of the Great Depression. Without the CWA, WPA and CCC, it may not have happened.

Had it not been for the "make-work" projects of President Franklin Roosevelt's original New Deal programs, towns all over America would have missed out on significant improvements. Everything, from art and research to highways, dams, parks and nature trails, was a product of the massive government effort during the 1930s to get Americans back to work. In Ashland, the Oregon Shakespeare Festival can be added to the list.

The festival's history, beginning eighty-five years ago, is well-known; yet, what may not be obvious is its original connection to New Deal projects. The federal government largesse played a significant role in providing the festival's founder, Angus Bowmer's, dream of turning an abandoned Chautauqua shell into a venue for Shakespearean performances. In his 1975 autobiography, Bowmer credited the Works Progress Administration (WPA) with the removal of the two old, sagging, domed wooden roofs of the worn and long-neglected Chautauqua building. Ashland's fire marshal ordered the domes removed in November 1933; it seems that Ashland youths had been jumping up and down on the partially collapsed wooden roofs, using it like a wonderful trampoline. Appalled by what he saw, the town's fire marshal saw the roofs as an accident waiting to happen. After all, those domes were 160 feet in diameter and built without pillars, trusses or steel. They were just strips of wood that had been nailed together with asbestos sheeting for waterproofing.

After the decapitation was ordered, eleven previously unemployed Ashland men were put to work by the Civilian Works Administration (CWA). The organization had been created in 1933 to address the widespread unemployment that was being experienced in the construction industry. Ashland's CWA was locally administered and later replaced in 1935 by the WPA that Bowmer had referred to. Nationally, the CWA employed four million people during its two-year existence. Whether it was called the CWA or the WPA at the time, the result was the same; only the circular cement walls that were once the base for the dome roof survived. Weeds had grown in the walls and chunks of them had flaked off since it had been abandoned. The massive structure that once welcomed opera singer Madame Schumann-Heink, populist presidential candidate William Jennings Bryan and fireball preacher and former baseball player Billy Sunday was reduced to a crumbling shell.

While some town boosters saw the site as a promising location for a sports stadium, Ashland Normal School professor Angus Bowmer and his friends had a different vision. Looking up from the park below, or from a high road well above, Bowmer noticed that the old shell had a striking similarity to the sketches of London's Globe Theatre. Bowmer thought: "Why not perform Shakespeare's plays inside the now-roofless Chautauqua walls?" He knew that he would need help to make the First Annual Shakespearean Festival happen.

The logo for one of President Franklin Roosevelt's New Deal programs, the Works Progress Administration. *Author's collection.*

Once again, unemployed Ashland men were put to work by a New Deal program. This time, their mission was to build a stage for Angus and his student actors. Ten men who worked for the WPA (successor to the CWA), who had previously been assigned to a street project, were reassigned to the theater project. Bowmer had convinced town officials that the idea of his festival might work; the town was, after all, in the middle of a devastating depression— anything might help. Over $1,000 in labor costs were eventually spent from relief funds.

With both the idea and the stage in place, yet another New Deal agency was called in to work on the project. Not everyone believed that the proposed Shakespeare festival would be financially successful or break even. A local citizens' committee, which was made up of town businessmen, proposed a daytime event for the newly built stage, just in case the evening performances were poorly attended. So, it was proposed that the stage should host boxing matches put on by the young men of the Medford-area Civilian Conservation Corps (CCC). Established two years earlier, the CCC provided work and vocational

Clothing patch for the Civilian Conservation Corps New Deal program. *Author's collection.*

training for unemployed, single young men who sought to conserve and develop natural resources. By 1935, five hundred thousand members were living in thousands of camps throughout the United States.

Obviously, Bowmer had designed his stage to be used for more refined entertainment, but he seemed unperturbed by the suggestion of the boxing matches. After all, theaters in Elizabethan England had used bearbaiting to draw a crowd, so what was the harm? Ironically, the CCC's onstage fisticuffs lost money, while the plays netted a small profit. In early July, 1935, for just fifty cents, Ashlanders were treated to performances of *Twelfth Night* on Friday evening and *The Merchant of Venice* on Saturday. Sunday night was reserved for a repeated performance of *Twelfth Night*. The forty-two rounds of CCC boxing became a kind of early "Green Show."

The list of the accomplishments of the original New Deal programs, both cherished and controversial, is long and well-documented. Thousands of towns benefited from all kinds of improvements, including improvements to hospitals, schools, roads, public buildings, bridges, parks, reservoirs, irrigation systems, sewers and sidewalks. In Ashland, Oregon, the programs' accomplishments also included the beginnings of a festival that, over time, forever changed and dominated the town's character and image.

20

They All Came to Ashland!

How is it that a small, rural town hundreds of miles from a major city was visited so many times by nationally well-known individuals?

Chautauqua and a Church Invitation

Best known for his involvement in the 1925 Scopes Monkey Trial, three-time Democratic presidential candidate William Jennings Bryan visited Ashland on three separate occasions: twice on the Chautauqua circuit and once at the personal request of his Ashland friends. The visits came between presidential runs and several years before his famous role as an anti-evolution activist in the Scopes Monkey Trial. Shortly after his first defeat to William McKinley in 1896, Bryan's appearance at Ashland's Chautauqua building attracted so many who wanted to hear "the great orator of Nebraska" in July 1897 that the session had to be moved outdoors to the adjoining park. Coming off a California tour, Bryan was exhausted and needed rest before his address. As prominent Ashland civic leaders, the McCalls offered Bryan a room in their Oak Street home, where he might be able to get some sleep before his speech. The next afternoon, beginning at 2:00 p.m., at least 2,500 people attended Bryan's frequently applauded, two-and-a-half-hour speech.

Immensely popular outside of the northeastern United States, Bryan spoke on the virtues of bimetallism—that is, the backing of paper dollars with both gold and silver. While this topic may seem like anything but a crowd-

Ashland visitor and three-time Democratic candidate for president, William Jennings Bryan's, campaign pin. *Author's collection.*

pleaser, it was a very appealing idea to farmers and debtors who would have benefited significantly from the government putting more paper money in circulation. Evidently, far less impressed by Bryan's speech, a rather hostile Ashland newspaper account made the assessment that "the great inflationist seems to have reached his expansion limits and will soon assume his normal condition as a local orator of mediocre talent in his native, cyclone-swept state of Nebraska."

In January 1907, a two-hour visit from Bryan resulted in much more favorable newspaper coverage in the *Ashland Tidings*. At the time of this visit, Bryan was California-bound, but his friends in Ashland encouraged him to make a brief stop in town. Once again, an overflowing crowd— estimated at 2,500 people—attended Bryan's lecture. The following day, the newspaper stated, "Mr. Bryan was in splendid form, speaking for an hour, and his address was both pleasing and instructive." Attendees said that he praised the greatness of America and was optimistic that the partisan divide that existed between the Democrats and Republicans at the time could be overcome. Bryan told the Ashland audience that the biggest problem facing the country was: "The great mass of the common people are not accumulating the riches of the country through their honest toil, but it is the men who have seized hold of the doors of commerce and trade and have monopolized them who have accumulated millions and are a menace to the country." Bryan made a similar speech that emphasized the dilemma of the nation's wealth in the hands of the few, in his 1919 Chautauqua circuit talk. The speech was preceded by a chicken dinner picnic and a greeting in Lithia Park, which he praised.

Next to the two presidents of his era who also visited Ashland, Teddy Roosevelt and Woodrow Wilson, many historians credit Ashland's controversial and somewhat frequent visitor, William Jennings Bryan, with being one of the most influential figures of the Progressive era. Interestingly, Bryan never carried the state of Oregon in any of his presidential bids. Oregon voted for William McKinley in 1896 and 1900 and for William Howard Taft in 1908.

On a Saturday evening, in the early spring of 1908, the citizens of Ashland didn't have to be members of the local congregation of Ashland's Methodist church on North Main Street to see and hear the foremost African American speaker in the country. Seating was free and open to all; although, there was a charge for people who wanted to sit in the prime reserved seats that were closer to the lectern. After all, the cost to bring a speaker of this caliber to town needed to at least be partially covered. On March 22, 1913, Booker T. Washington addressed a full house of fascinated valley residents who had come to see and hear the only black man who had ever been invited to the White House for dinner and who often spoke at prestigious eastern locations, including Madison Square Garden and Carnegie Hall. Washington was widely known as a leading educator of the late nineteenth and early twentieth centuries.

In anticipation of the event, the *Ashland Tidings*'s editor made a strong argument for attending and contributing financially to the speech so that the original organizers, including G.F. Billings, an Ashland businessman and church member, would not have "to dig down in their pockets to pay a deficit." The editor explained that Washington required a $125 speaking fee, plus local expenses, but they closed the preview article optimistically by stating, "Ashland people generally do the right thing in such matters. Come." And come they did. At this time, most had heard of Washington's efforts to educate the South's former slaves, and some had possibly read his 1903 autobiography *Up from Slavery*. Washington's approach to racial issues was nonconfrontational and focused on self-help through education. As a supporter of the Republican Party and a moderate civil rights leader, Washington had advised both President Roosevelt and President Taft on racial issues. He maintained that cooperation with supportive white leaders, especially those in the North, was the only way to overcome racism in the long run.

It is not surprising that his emphasis on education throughout his speech in Ashland was well-received, as the town was known for being firmly committed to reestablishing its own normal school. Washington explained how his students actually built their own school at the Tuskegee Institute in Alabama. While his school's goal of producing teachers was the same as Ashland's, he stressed that both male and female students had to learn trades alongside academics. His students, who were going to return to the rural South, needed additional skills. He explained that students learned how to make bricks, construct classrooms and outbuildings, grow their own crops and raise livestock at Tuskegee.

An *Ashland Daily Tidings* writer, who was commenting on Washington's visit, gushed, "Dr. Washington is a great man, doing great work." He continued, "Born in slavery and rising from an ignorant helper in a West Virginia coal mine to one of the leading educators of the world, regardless of race, his record is something to be proud of." Upon Washington's return to Alabama, he wrote a thank-you note to Ashland rancher and businessman G.F. Billings for his initial invite and the "extreme kindness to [him] while in [the] city." In the note, he said, "I hope, at some time, we can welcome you as a visitor to this institution." Unfortunately, Washington died two short years after his Ashland visit, at the age of fifty-nine.

In July 1919, valley residents had the opportunity to see and hear, within a few days, two famous speakers discuss the recent war and peace settlement. Fiery evangelist and former major-league baseball player Billy Sunday preached an opening service and lectured at Ashland's twenty-sixth Chautauqua event. A speech from Ida Tarbell, the leading progressive reform journalist, sometimes referred to as a "Muckraker" due to her best-selling exposé of the Standard Oil Company monopoly, was also scheduled. Huge banner advertisements were taken out in the local papers for Billy Sunday's coming appearance, warning people to buy tickets in advance. They stated, "After sufficient tickets have been sold to fill the building, no more will be issued, so plan to buy your tickets early. There is going to be a big crowd. The auditorium will be filled to its capacity." Tarbell apparently lacked Sunday's advance men, as her lecture "Our Nation, Its Problems and Progress" was simply listed as one of several notable speeches to be given.

By the time of Sunday's Ashland visit, he had a paid staff of twenty-six people—a far cry from his humble beginnings, which he partially spent in an orphanage. His athleticism, though, was noticed early on, and it eventually led him to a professional baseball contract with the Chicago White Stockings (today's Chicago Cubs) of the National Baseball League. Sunday played

Booker T. Washington lectured at Ashland's Methodist church to an over-flow crowd in 1913. *Courtesy of Southern Oregon Historical Society.*

centerfield for three different teams over an eight-year career, and he was best known for his base-stealing and acrobatic diving catches, which fans loved to watch. He played in the era before gloves were widely used by outfielders, so his catches had to be made barehanded.

Likely influenced by gospel mission encounters, in 1891, Sunday requested a release from his baseball contract so that he could pursue a "born-again life" as a preacher. Aside from his Chautauqua appearances, Sunday held big-city revival meetings, where he preached "old-time religion" in a very entertaining and animated way. Falling back on his baseball background, Sunday would mimic sliding into home plate, or he would take the role of an umpire calling someone out. On stage, he would leave the lectern, run, jump and act out the fate of those who were unsaved in what he deemed God's judgment. Several mainline religious figures criticized his antics, especially his use of slang. Crowds, including the reported three thousand he drew in Ashland, were, nevertheless, enthusiastic followers of his more dramatic presentations.

Sunday's Ashland lecture emphasized the recent world war, the German kaiser and his thoughts regarding the League of Nations. He made it clear to his audience that he was a passionate supporter of the Great War, and he argued that it was a fight of "hell against heaven"—the United States was fighting "Christ's war." Sunday had raised large sums of money for the cause by selling war bonds, and he had been involved in recruitment drives. In what was tactfully described as his vivid vocabulary, Sunday described what he thought should be done with the German kaiser. The Ashland audience "heartily endorsed" his comments, according to newspaper accounts. In regard to the League of Nations, Sunday said he favored it but only "insofar as it does not conflict with nationalism and the Monroe Doctrine." If it did, Sunday stated, "I'll be darned if I'll vote for it." Once again, the Ashland crowd showed its approval with the waving of their handkerchiefs, which was called the "Chautauqua Salute."

Barely back from Paris and the peace conference she had recently attended, Ida Tarbell "brought back with her many vivid impressions of this great event," explained a local Ashland reporter. Tarbell's accounts of war-torn France and her concerns about the terms that had been handed to Germany were large parts of her lecture. Paris had always been important to her, as she had lived and studied there in the earlier years of her life. At the time of her speech in Ashland, Tarbell had witnessed, firsthand, the massive devastation of World War I, and it deeply saddened her. She explained to her audience that, while America was lightly touched by the world war, France received the full brunt of it. Nearly 1.5 million young French men did not return, and Tarbell stressed that many others had returned so physically wounded that they would be unable to support their families. As Tarbell walked the streets of her beloved Paris, she noted that only a few shops were open for business after four years of war and disorder—many had simply become bombed-out ruins. Paris, Tarbell said, had to be restored for the sake of world civilization. Typical of the investigative style of journalism Ida was famous for, she interviewed Parisians about how the war had affected them, and, then, she traveled to the countryside and interviewed farmers who lived on what was left of their properties. Tarbell explained that she was most interested in the fate of the average Frenchman and Frenchwoman.

Speaking of the peace treaty settlement itself, Tarbell said, "The terms for Germany were too harsh and will, in time, mean another World War." Interestingly, President Wilson had wanted Tarbell to be in the official American delegation, but Wilson's then-secretary of state, Robert Lansing, refused to have a female in his delegation. On the issue of the League of Nations, Tarbell was a crusader for American involvement, without Billy Sunday's caveat regarding national sovereignty. These two famous Chautauqua circuit speakers, disparate in so many other ways, both heaped profuse praise on America's "doughboys" and worked tirelessly for the war effort. Tarbell maintained that the Chautauqua talks, including hers and Sunday's, brought "a fresh element into the social life of a small town, providing stimulating ideas that the country must understand and study."

A Shakespeare Festival Training Ground

The Oregon Shakespeare Festival (OSF) doesn't talk about its success much; after all, it is a reparatory theater. While curtain calls are taken together, a couple dozen actors from the OSF have gone on to television, movie and theater success, causing some to characterize OSF as an incubator for talent. In many cases, Ashland audiences have had the opportunity to see actors develop their craft early in their careers—well before their many awards and public acclaims.

Seven years after George Peppard played Hamlet's friend Horatio on Ashland's outdoor stage, he starred in *Breakfast at Tiffany's*, alongside Audrey

Hepburn. Peppard spent three summers in Ashland in the early 1950s. Over his long career, he was also known as "Bannack" and Hannibal Smith on television's *The A-Team* in the 1980s.

Dick Cavett's very brief appearance at OSF in 1956 somewhat personifies the early repertory nature of Ashland's theater, as he appeared in no less than seven minor roles in the five plays that were offered that August. The popular talk show host of *The Dick Cavett Show* (1969 to present in various formats) has won three Emmy awards and was nominated for many more.

Stacy Keach spent the summers of 1962 and 1963 on the Ashland stage, "deepening [his] knowledge of and the appreciation for Shakespeare" in six roles. He said, "I got paid fifty dollars a week, and we rehearsed one play in the morning, another in the afternoon and the third in the evening." This intensity, he said, gave him an appreciation for repertory theater, because it was a great training ground for young actors. It was his title role in OSF's *Henry V* that led to the glowing review that gave him his first national press

Stacy Keach in the 1963 Ashland, Oregon Shakespeare performance that garnered him national attention. *Courtesy of Stacy Keach and the Oregon Shakespeare Festival.* Henry V, *1963.*

attention in 1963. Keach's awards and roles have been numerous. Well known for his countless television, film and theater portrayals, he is perhaps best known as detective Mike Hammer, or more recently, as Ken Titus. He has been inducted into the Theatre Hall of Fame and has a star on the Hollywood Walk of Fame.

Only in residence for one year at OSF, William Hurt has been one of the festival's most successful "graduates." As a winner of a best actor academy award for *Kiss of the Spider Woman*, he has been nominated for other performances, including his roles in *Children of a Lesser God*, *Broadcast News* and *A History of Violence*. Hurt was cast in *Long Day's Journey into Night* and *Henry VI, Part one* on the Elizabethan stage in the summer of 1975.

While Peppard, Cavett, Keach and Hurt all spent time in Ashland early in their careers, Anthony Heald came to OSF in 1995, as an established and successful Broadway actor, who had already earned two Tony Award nominations. His friends were somewhat shocked that he gave up New York for Ashland, but he decided that he could raise his family in the small town and act where audiences showed great respect for the art. The OSF has become a "vibrant leader in the national theatre scene." Heald pointed out, "The fact that you're an actor in the festival carries weight." Outside of Broadway and Ashland, Heald is likely best known for his role as Dr. Frederick Chilton in *The Silence of the Lambs* and as Scott Gruber on television's *Boston Public*. He continues to perform annually in a wide variety of roles in the festival's three theaters, to the delight of Ashland's receptive audiences.

Many more of the festival's actors have gone on to television, movie and stage fame, including Jean Smart (*Designing Women*), Kyle MacLachlan (*Twin Peaks*), James Avery (*Fresh Prince of Bel-Air*), Gretchen Corbett (*Rockford Files*), Harry Anderson (*Night Court*), Monte Markham (*Melrose Place*) and Dennis Arndt (*Heisenberg*). They all played parts in Ashland before gaining a national audience.

21

The "Miracle Woman" Comes to Town

For thirty years, Susie Jessel was the most famous person in town, and she arguably had the biggest business!

Before the GI Bill filled Ashland's small college with students—and while the town's Shakespeare Festival was silent during World War II—Susie Jessel was a one-person attraction, filling Ashland hotels, motels and auto camps with pilgrims in search of her health-giving touch. Today, most people associate Ashland, Oregon, with its Shakespeare festival and Southern Oregon University. But Susie was the reason that thousands flocked to this small town from the early 1930s well into the 1960s—she put Ashland on the map. It also didn't hurt that *True Magazine* ran a glowing multipage article on the faith healer, complete with photos, right in the middle of World War II. The article caused some to speculate that Jessel was the economic wartime force that kept numerous Ashland businesses afloat. Susie, herself, attributed the overwhelming influx of hundreds of new patients to Ashland from around the United States, Canada and Mexico with the 1943 publication of her work in *True Magazine*. So many came seeking relief that it became necessary for her to build a village of small cabins on the Jessel property in order to accommodate everyone who wanted to be treated by an individual with a fourth-grade education and no medical training.

In her day, Jessel was referred to as a faith healer; today, she may have been known as a practitioner of alternative medicine. But Jessel may have been

Susie Jessel comes to Ashland. *Courtesy of Southern Oregon Historical Society.*

troubled by that description. As she stated in her magazine article, Jessel took no payment for her treatments; she kept no books, made no appointments, knew few patients by name and saw up to five hundred people per week. She maintained that her gift of healing came from God, yet she did not indulge in any kind of religious fervor. Put simply, Susie attributed her ability to heal about 80 percent of her patients to her being an instrument of God.

K.R. Ellis, the author of the *True Magazine* feature on Jessel, admitted that he arrived in Ashland extremely skeptical. How could this country healer be so successful? She saw patients when traditional medicine had been unsuccessful, and most of her patients had little hope of a traditional cure. Ellis needed to find out how Jessel worked. Because there were always long lines of her faithful patients awaiting additional treatments, Ellis took his opportunity to interview them, and he soon had a notebook full of stories. He admitted that the average person might find the accounts fantastic, so he needed to probe further and get testimony from those who had been treated by her in the past. This resulted in countless more stories of once hopeless— and then cured—individuals who eagerly signed affidavits to that effect.

Ellis realized that these accounts were also limited. He needed to seek some views from the outside. He found that the Ashland Chamber of Commerce was handing out flattering accounts of her work that had been extracted from numerous newspaper articles. Local doctors were less enthusiastic and attributed her successes to faith alone, so it was, consequently, limited. After several days in Ashland, Ellis was left with a dilemma; he either had to accept the stories he had heard firsthand, or he had to conclude everybody was a liar.

But there was more. Dr. Charles Mayo of the Rochester Mayo Clinic had previously visited Ashland in an effort to find out how Jessel had been able to do what he was unable to do for one of his most difficult cases. In addition to this account, Eleanor Roosevelt had urged Mrs. Jessel to come to Warm Springs, Georgia, due to Susie's success in treating paralysis cases. The country of Switzerland also offered to pay all of Jessel's expenses and provide a sanitarium for her use if she would travel there. But Susie declined this and countless other offers, indicating that she had all she needed in her enlarged treatment room on Idaho Street in the village of Ashland, Oregon.

No wonder the *True Magazine* article made Susie Jessel even more famous, both nationally and internationally. Ashland's motels, restaurants and rooming houses were filled with those who sought Jessel's healing. Ellis, who admitted he came to Ashland as a skeptic and an investigator, was given exclusive time with Jessel to observe and photograph her treatments and interview whomever he wanted. What's more, Jessel cured Ellis of a pain in his side within five treatments that each lasted a few minutes. Ellis didn't try to conclude how significant or scientific Susie's successes were, but the overall testimonial nature of the article, with scores of specific examples, said plenty.

Years later, a 1953 *Time Magazine* article was less kind to Jessel. It dwelt on how much money she was said to have brought in through individual donations and the renting of her cabins, where patients could stay as they awaited additional treatments. The article even included snide comments about how the local undertaker buried eighteen of her patients in a single year and how a dying man would grab at anything.

Born in 1891 in the rural South, Susie was a devoutly religious person who was said to have a special gift. There are numerous accounts of her healing powers, even from when she was a young girl. There are also many accounts of her infatuation with a state in the Far West—Oregon. She loved geography and decided, at an early age, that she would somehow live in Oregon. Eventually, with her extended family in tow, Jessel moved to Baker, Oregon, at the urging of an old family friend; there, she settled in, treating locals on request. One of her neighbors needed her to treat her father who lived in Grants Pass, and this trip offered her the opportunity to see the nearby Rogue Valley town that numerous people had previously told her about.

Jessel had heard of a beautiful little town named Ashland, but she had also heard that there was no work or money there. Undeterred, Susie wanted to see southern Oregon and decide for herself whether the town she had heard so much about was a viable option for her. At first sight, Jessel concluded that Ashland was clean and, likely, a nice place to raise her family. What impressed her most about the town was its education system. A child could go from the first grade all the way through college in the same town. A year later, the Jessels moved to 517 Iowa Street in Ashland.

Susie's husband, Charlie, found that the stories about no work in Ashland were true. After becoming desperate, he applied to work for the New Deal Works Progress Administration, but he found that local officials favored giving those jobs to long-term residents first. Susie, skeptical of the new program to begin with, decided to look into it herself. In a lively confrontation with the administrator at city hall, Jessel told him to either give her husband a job or shoot the entire family, including Charlie and Susie's six children. Two days later, Charlie had a job digging and burning poison oak in Lithia Park.

Meanwhile, Ashland's citizens were hearing of Mrs. Jessel's hands-on healing, and many were still coming for treatments from eastern Oregon. In need of a break, the family decided to winter in Phoenix, Arizona, but

"Miracle Woman" Jessel's "hands-on healing." *Author's collection.*

soon found that her patients had followed her south. Several even moved to Ashland permanently to be nearby, and it was not unusual for a patient to stay in the area for months at a time. On her return to Ashland, Susie found that her cottages had been vandalized; furniture had been stolen, and it took months to restore the properties. The Jessels had no further extended vacations.

Trouble came to the Jessels in other ways as well. Despite general acceptance from the religious community of Ashland, her own Baptist church expelled her for "teaching heresy." This, Susie pointed out, came after twenty years of faithful attendance and commitment to the church. Even a number of local ministers opposed her excommunication. Additionally, Susie admitted that her success may have caused envy in certain quarters, as some fostered the idea that she was "rolling in money" while avoiding income tax. Several letters were sent to the IRS, and soon, the Jessels were under investigation for failure to pay tax on income. Susie was told that two town doctors were behind what she referred to as the "poison-pen letters."

Uneducated in these matters, the Jessels sought a tax attorney, who finally was able to settle the claims for them. The mental and financial strain of the investigation took its toll. As Susie pointed out, the patients who came to her had little money, and in some cases, she financed their ability to stay in town for treatments. She never charged and only received small donations that usually consisted of a dollar or small change that was discretely slipped into the front pocket of her apron. Once again, her naiveté may have been partially responsible for her troubles. Jessel believed she was simply doing the work of God and couldn't understand people who would want to hurt others.

On June 16, 1966, Susie Jessel died of natural causes at the age of seventy-five. The local newspaper described her passing as the end of an era in Ashland. An overflowing crowd flooded her funeral services at Litwiller Chapel, and her planned, simple graveside service in the Ashland cemetery resulted in another large gathering of mourners. Her obituary pointed out that she was both renowned and the subject of criticism. It seems that Susie Jessel was controversial to the end.

Reluctantly, two of Susie's children carried on her work at the treatment room on Idaho Street. Of her six children, only Joe and Alma Jessel felt that they had the same gift of healing that their mother possessed, but neither was enthusiastic about taking on the task. They witnessed their mother work as many as eighteen hours a day, and she had little time for them. Consequently, both chose to see far fewer patients each day. Joe carried on until his death in 1975. Alma moved back to Ashland upon Joe's passing and applied her healing hands to the business well into the 1980s. The Jessel house on Holly Street is currently operated as a "traveler's accommodation" by Tim Rutter, who purchased the property from one of the Jessel sisters in 1987. Rutter thinks that, whether you believe Susie had the power to heal or not, a very significant thing happened during her time in Ashland. All of the people she brought to town helped support the community during a long period of difficult times.

PART VIII
A BRUSH WITH HISTORY

Yesterday is history.
—Bill Keane

22

President Lincoln Has Lost His Head Again, and Pioneer Mike Is Missing His Hand and Gun!

Between 1910 and 1929, four statues and fountains were erected in Ashland as memorials to members of the pioneer generation.

Currently, towns across America are struggling over what to do with their century-old pieces of public art from a different time. Often, the issues with these monuments revolve around the appropriateness of them in an era with different sensibilities. Heroic Civil War monuments and certain depictions of Native Americans have particularly come under attack, as each generation interprets the past differently. However, whether or not these sites should be viewed through the lens of the past or the standards of the present, this has not been an issue in Ashland. Rather, sheer vandalism and, to some degree, neglect seem to be the challenges that Ashland's vintage memorials face.

Abraham Lincoln turned down the chance to be the territorial governor of Oregon, he never traveled farther west than Kansas and he only won 38 percent of Oregon's presidential vote. So, why has a statue of him become such a piece of folklore in Ashland? Dedicated in 1916 to the memory of one of Ashland's pioneers, a standing marble statue of Abraham Lincoln has been beheaded four times.

Purchased at the San Francisco Panama Pacific Exposition in 1915, and crafted in Antonio Frilli's Florence, Italy studio, the statue of Lincoln has lost its head four times in a continuing cycle of decapitation, lengthy storage, creation of a new head, replacement in Lithia Park and, once again,

Left: The Abraham Lincoln statute in Lithia Park is a constant victim of vandalism. *Courtesy of Southern Oregon Historical Society.*

Right: The Lincoln statute is kept in Lithia Park's storage for safekeeping—although it is less than dignified. *Author's collection.*

decapitation. Essentially left alone until 1958, when it was initially toppled over by young vandals, the statue has been in and out of repair ever since. Its storage location is almost as bizarre as its beheading. Whether it has been lying headless in the weeds at the sewer treatment plant or actually buried below ground behind the Butler bandstand, the statue's storage has been less than noble while it has awaited its next new head.

Ashland businessman Gwin Butler attended the San Francisco exposition and was fascinated with the idea of buying a Lincoln statue and a fountain he saw there. He planned to have the pieces shipped to Ashland, where they would be in place for the 1916 Lithia Park dedication on the hillside land that he and fellow businessman Domingo Perrozi had recently donated for the park's expansion purposes. After joining Butler at the exposition, Domingo, too, thought the fountain would be a fitting entry piece for the much enlarged park. Gwin paid $2,500 ($65,000 in 2020 dollars) for the Lincoln statue, and both Butler and Perrozi bought the peach-colored marble fountain for $3,000 ($74,000 in 2020 dollars). The fountain featured a swan and winged cherub, with pools below. The railroad's freight charges for the pieces cost extra.

Butler sought to honor his stepfather, pioneer Jacob Thompson, with the Lincoln statue and had a four-foot-high granite base built and engraved for the five-foot-two white marble statue to stand on. Butler had lost his father to suicide at the tender age of five, and a few years later, Gwin's mother married Thompson, who Gwin idolized growing up. Thompson was known as a politically strong "Union" man, which may have been why Butler chose to honor his stepfather with the statue of the sixteenth president.

As previously stated, the Lincoln sculpture has suffered a number of indignities over the years, including additional beheadings in 1967 and 1973, after the first 1958 episode. Once it was repaired, the statue was relocated, from the knoll adjoining the Butler-Perrozi fountain to the stairway leading to the Shakespeare festival grounds, in hopes that it would be more visible and a less-likely target of vandals. Unfortunately, the change of location didn't work. After a significant effort by Ashland sculptor Jeffrey Bernard to craft another head, complete with a 1991 city dedication ceremony, Lincoln was, again, headless by 2005. A new head, which was crafted in China and attached with a rod, was sawed through in 2008, leaving the statue in need of significant repair once again. The statue currently stands headless in a park warehouse, but the granite base remains in place, statue-less.

Three Lincoln heads are currently kept in Lithia Park's storage. *Author's collection.*

The fountain has suffered from both vandalism and simple neglect over time. In fact, by the 1980s, it had to be rediscovered. Lithia Park fell on hard times for decades, with little money available for park maintenance, despite the best efforts of park staff and volunteers. The town simply had too little income and many pressing needs. By the 1960s, many citizens avoided the park all together, as counterculture transients had practically taken up residence there. Two major floods later added to the dilemma. It wasn't until the 1980s that deferred maintenance could be addressed, including the restoration of the Butler-Perrozi Fountain.

Today, with the fountain in clear view, it is hard to imagine that it was buried under thick brush and had to be rediscovered in 1981. John Fregonese, Ashland's planning director in the 1980s, cut away blackberry bushes and led a lengthy restoration project, along with Jeffrey Bernard and Dennis DeBey, which culminated in a July 4, 1987 rededication ceremony. Fregonese family members started a foundation in 2018 in order to raise the funds for a much-needed restoration of the fountain complex in John's memory.

Ashland's first and oldest pioneer memorial, which was prominently placed in the downtown plaza in 1910, has had a similar history of vandalism and repair. Known affectionately as "Pioneer Mike," the fountain has also had to withstand the elements for 110 years. The fountain itself is known as the Carter Memorial Fountain and was a gift to the city from the children of Henry and Harriet Carter. The Carters were very successful early business entrepreneurs. Originally, the design was a cast-iron drinking fountain with twelve individual bubbling fountains and four bowl-like troughs for horses and dogs at its base. Atop the elaborate water fountain a five-foot-two-inch cast-zinc statue of a pioneer peers east, holding his rifle at his side.

Four such statues with different bases were ordered by various towns from a New York ironworks between 1903 and 1912. Currently, only the statues in Storm Lake, Iowa, and Ashland are still standing. Hit by a truck in 1931, the Ashland statue and fountain required repair and some modifications. Not unlike the fountains in Lithia Park, vandals have made it difficult to keep the plaza pioneer figure in place over the years, beginning in the late 1960s, when "Mike" was roped and pulled down. More indignities occurred over the next fifteen years. The statue itself became a kind of "jungle gym," with a pattern of breakage, removal, repair and reinstallation atop the fountain.

After a 2014 vandalism incident that resulted in significant damage to the pioneer figure, the city hired George Kramer, a historic preservation consultant, to prepare a report with options to consider. Kramer found that

The library is the current location of the winged cherub that stood above the Butler-Perrozi fountain. *Author's collection.*

A cast-bronze replica of the pioneer statute atop a plaza fountain. *Photograph courtesy of Terry Skibby.*

it was possible to make a mold and create a replication of "Pioneer Mike" using the Storm Lake statue. Somewhat surprisingly, the City of Storm Lake had no objections. His recommendation was to recast "Mike" in bronze, thereby significantly increasing its strength and reinforcing the fountain below. At the time of this book's writing, a cast-bronze replica of the original pioneer looks out from the plaza, toward the eastern route that ushered in the early pioneer generation.

Still, another pioneer fountain figure looks east from her base in front of the Ashland Carnegie Library on the corner of Gresham Street and Siskiyou Boulevard. Erected in 1929 as the result of a will bequest, a statute

Michelson Chapman Memorial Fountain in front of Ashland Library. *Photograph courtesy of Terry Skibby.*

of a woman holding a torch stands atop a granite and marble fountain. For the first several years of its existence, the statue dispensed both regular water and Lithia water from four individual fountains. These fountains malfunctioned relatively early on and were closed off, yet the statue has remained in place without the vandalism issues of other Ashland pioneer memorials. It has mainly suffered from neglect during its ninety-one years of outdoor exposure.

Upon her death in 1928, eighty-four-year-old Victoria Mickelson-Chapman willed all of the proceeds from her assets to be committed to the erection of a fountain and statue in memory of her two pioneer families.

It was to be a gift to the city. "*They Lighted the Way,* Michelson Chapman Memorial Fountain" was to be engraved in the marble base. The female figure holds her torch down, extinguishing it in the water—likely a symbol of death. The memorial cost just under $4,000 to build ($57,000 in 2020 dollars). Whether the Italian marble sculpture was meant to be a representation of a pioneer woman or the biblical Rebekah has long been a subject of speculation. Victoria's will gives no clues. Her only instructions read, "A suitable life-sized statute is to be placed at the top."

While Ashland's struggle to maintain its historical memorials has not suffered the political rancor of other parts of the country; their abilities to be cost-effective and historically minded at the same time have proven to be significant challenges. Deciding how long public money and energy should maintain and protect what were initially privately funded century-old gifts will likely be an ongoing debate of a different sort. Historic preservation is always open to new interpretations, and deciding on what to preserve and what to let go is part of that process.

23

Urban Legends Die Hard

Urban legends are easy to believe and difficult to dispel, especially where many single men reside in rooming houses "on the wrong side of town."

A town's history is often clouded with all sorts of misrepresentations or unintentional mistakes, which can contribute to long-lasting debatable stories. One does not need to look very far in the once booming part of Ashland called the railroad district to find an example. Assertions continue to be made regarding the history of a once modest, surviving rooming house on Fourth Street. Today, the 120-year-old restored structure is a thriving bed-and-breakfast resort, which is, ironically, at least partially responsible for the more recent revival of this part of town.

Why do some stories persist? One explanation may simply be that urban legends die hard. Rooted in local popular culture and often presented as true, these tales become modern folklore. Once a story from what appears to be a reasonable source gets embedded in the minds of listeners, it is hard to dispel. Urban myths often provide us with convenient, coherent and convincing explanations of life in the past. After all, wasn't every boardinghouse with inexpensive, small rooms in a working-class community a brothel?

Then, there is a story's plausibility, as some are based in fact. Following the completion of the north–south railroad link over the steep Siskiyou Mountains in 1887, Ashland became a division point for the Southern Pacific Railroad, which resulted in the creation of a whole new business center along Fourth Street, near the 1888 depot. Various enterprises, including cafés, a grocery store, a drugstore, a bakery, a pool hall, a butcher shop, laundries, several bars, many rooming houses and at least one documented brothel, sprang up to provide services for travelers and the mostly single, male railroad employees. The developing area, which was removed from the rest of commercial Ashland, soon required both its own fire station and jail. The town's original, and larger, business district was a mile away from the railroad district, along Ashland Creek and Main Street, which was often referred to as the boulevard. Those who lived and worked 'below the boulevard," near Fourth Street, were generally seen as living in a much coarser world.

Suddenly, forty years of railroad-created economic prosperity evaporated. With the 1927 decision to divert the main Shasta Southern Pacific route through Klamath Falls, Ashland's railroad district rapidly declined. Within a few years, even the depot was torn down, along with a number of other buildings and businesses, leaving the area as a neglected backwater for decades. With only one surviving former boardinghouse on the once bustling Fourth Street, it has been easy to generalize about boardinghouses and what took place at Peerless Rooms.

Fined $100 For Failure to Eject

E. B. Shaw, owner of the Fairview rooming house on Fourth street, was fined $100 in police court Wednesday for failure to eject Mrs. Eva Pierce within ten days of receiving notice to do so. He was notified May 7, following conviction of Mrs. Pierce on a charge of running a house of ill-fame. City Attorney Moore conducted the prosecution, Chief of Police Atterbury supplying the details of testimony. Mr. Shaw was represented by Attorney Kelly of Medford. The jury consisted of W. H. Cowdy, J. J. Murphy, A. W. Storey, H. T. Elmore, Howard Rose and J. H. McGee.

Ashland newspaper article indicating that Eva Pierce was running an illegal business at the Fairview Rooming House, not the Peerless, which was a block away. *Courtesy of the Terry Skibby collection.*

Are the urban tales about the former Peerless an example of unintentional mistaken identity? Was the well-known Madam Eva Pierce "working" there as it has been asserted and repeated over time? Based on her arrest records, it appears not to be the case. Just a half block up the street, on the corner of Fourth and B streets, was the site of one of the several other boardinghouses that operated near the Peerless. Named the Fairview, it was there that "Big Eva" operated her enterprise. Owner E.B. Shaw was even fined one hundred dollars by the local city court after she failed to remove her business from his building in June 1917. Meanwhile, Mrs.

Pierce, a major contributor to the Red Cross and town Liberty Fund Drive, was convicted of "running a house of ill-fame" at the Fairview.

It appears that the real history of the Peerless Rooms has been unfairly tainted by rumor and the fact that it is still standing, while the Fairview was torn down during an ill-fated urban removal project of the 1960s and 1970s. To be sure, the Peerless was both home to a commercial operation and a boardinghouse, but it was a barbershop operated by the same man from 1911 to 1951. Called the Mirror Barbershop, due to its vertically attached mirror between the two front doors, Samuel S. Davies cut hair on the lower floor through both good times and the hard times that followed the railroad diversion and the Great Depression.

Long abandoned after Davies's tenure, Peerless Rooms had become a dilapidated eyesore, with a faded 1915 Coca-Cola advertisement painted

The nationally recognized and completely transformed Peerless Bed-and-Breakfast Inn today. *Photograph courtesy of Terry Skibby.*

on one side as its only redeeming feature. Apparently undaunted, a couple who recently moved to Ashland from Hawaii, Crissy and Steve Barnett, purchased the former boardinghouse and barbershop. The pair had witnessed marginal neighborhoods in Honolulu become upscale spaces and wondered why this couldn't happen in Ashland's much-neglected railroad district. A serious investment of time and money followed. The building needed nearly everything redone, including a new foundation, structural work, rewiring, plumbing and heating and air conditioning.

The result of the couple's purchase and remodel was a complete transformation. The building now contains six luxury rooms with private baths, rather than the original fourteen with a bath down the hall. Formerly used to house railroad workers and traveling salesmen, the remodeled structure now functions as a bed and breakfast. Fortunately for the much maligned and neglected former boardinghouse and barbershop, its owners have renewed the structure and even successfully sought National Historical designation.

Samuel Davies, not Eva Pierce, is the person and legacy that should be remembered at the Peerless Rooming House. Davies's business kept him busy as both a barber on the main floor and a room keeper upstairs. He labored until his death in 1951, despite economic depression all around him. An urban myth may be more interesting and titillating than barber Davies, but it can also obscure what actually took place.

24

THE DAY ASHLAND ALMOST BURNED!

There was a state centennial anniversary to celebrate, and a brand-new $275,000 theater building just opened at the Shakespeare Festival grounds. Standby for evacuation?

In the Shakespearean play *Antony and Cleopatra*, Cleopatra's dying words include her exclamation that she is "fire and air." Performed the night of August 8, 1959, on Ashland's new Elizabethan stage, it is hard to imagine a more ironic line. Hundreds of acres of trees were bursting into flames, and the fire was being blown by intense winds on a ridge just above the theater as actress Barbara Waide was uttering those words. Both Ashland's Lithia Park and its just-completed theater were in the path of a massive wildfire the likes of which no one had seen in Ashland for nearly fifty years.

An arson fire that spread to four thousand acres threatened Ashland's only water supply, its signature park, Granite Street, its Shakespeare festival grounds and, possibly, the town's very existence. Two small brush fires had been separately set that morning above Jackson Hot Springs and on Ashland Mine Road; the fires quickly merged, spreading rapidly and dangerously on track to ignite homes above the city and its watershed. In the early stages of the fire, fourteen aerial attacks had been carried out with a borate solution, but they had done little to slow the blaze. The *Ashland Tidings* account of the day identified three stages of reaction in town. Despite numerous reports of wildfires in neighboring California, many citizens just didn't believe that they

The 1959 forest fire as seen from the downtown plaza. *Photograph courtesy of Terry Skibby.*

could happen here. In fact, by midday, for large numbers of folks, the billows of smoke became a kind of "spectator entertainment" as they went about their business on the plaza and watched from neighboring hills. However, by dusk, numerous residents were either preparing for evacuation or had already left their homes.

A wildfire of this potential consequence had not ravaged the Ashland Watershed since 1910. Besides Roseburg, Oregon, just to the north of Ashland, was the news of the day. The town had suffered an enormous explosion, killing fourteen and completely leveling four square blocks, just a day before the Ashland fire. A parked truck filled with chemicals, tons of dynamite and ammonium nitrate had shattered a section of downtown Roseburg, creating a mushroom cloud and fifty-foot crater that was twenty feet deep. For most Oregonians, Roseburg, Oregon, was, understandably, the breaking news of August 8—until later in the day, when the wildfire threat became real to previous spectators.

And, then, there were the celebrations. Around 1,100 people attended the Lithia Park party that was known as "Feasting at the Tribe of Will." The year 1959 was a new beginning for the town, with both a state centennial and new theater building to enjoy. For over a week, the big story in Ashland had been the grand opening of the Elizabethan Theatre and the record number of playgoers who came to see what was billed as "the finest Shakespeare theatre in the world." Both movie star Ginger Rogers and Oregon governor Mark Hatfield were in town to help dedicate the theater on July 28. A special feature acknowledging Oregon history and statehood was performed that evening, along with Shakespearean plays. Built in just eleven months, and only after a huge fundraising effort, the new theater had hosted five plays in rotation between its dedication night and September 5. What started as a sales slogan by the festival nearly became a mantra for theater goers: "stay four days, see four plays." It meant that the actors had to perform the plays seven nights a week, in rotation. Actress Peggy Rubin remembered, "We didn't cancel plays in those days." *Antony and Cleopatra* was performed every four days, and Saturday, September 8, was the cast's third performance. Even with very visible dense pillars of multicolored smoke above the ridge, right beyond the theater and town, a packed house experienced the play they had come to see. Bill Patton, the festival's general manager was assured by the fire marshal that if the blaze broke through Lithia Park to the north that word would be given so that theatergoers could get to their cars and evacuate. For the time being, however, the play was helping the fire department keep traffic off the streets, even as the town's scenic backdrop was exploding.

Many residents had already packed their bags. Those who lived along Ashland Mine Road, where the blaze had started, had already left their homes, as did those who lived in the Lithia Auto Camp and Trailer Park. After packing everything of value into their cars, the lead actors of *Antony and Cleopatra*, Theodore Marcuse and Barbara Waide, left the auto camp, unsure that they would have cabins to return to. The residents of Grandview and Strawberry Lane drenched their land and homes in water, hoping it would protect their properties and crops.

Also on stage that night, playing Cleopatra's handmaidens, were Shirley Patton and Margaret Vafiadis (Rubin). Both have clear memories of performing with the roaring noise of the nearby blaze and trees exploding like Roman candles. Projecting over all of this noise to a large and constantly distracted audience was difficult, at best. When not on stage, the actors gathered on the back deck to monitor how close the fire had come since they had last looked. Everyone was extremely alert; Shirley remembered, "That night, no one missed their entrances." Both Peggy and Shirley were fascinated that they could see the audience's faces so clearly at an evening performance. They remember that the audience members' faces looked like bright red tomatoes, illuminated by the reflection of the flames on the ridge above. With the final scene completed, the audience gave the cast a standing ovation and headed for their cars. The male cast members changed out of their costumes and joined the hundreds of firefighters, who were, by then, assembled in the upper section of Lithia Park. Fortunately, the wind direction had started to change.

The winds, which had gotten up to speeds of thirty miles per hour, had been fanning the flames during the 105-degree-Fahrenheit day, resulting in the incineration of, at one point, 1,000 acres in a single hour. Over 4,000 acres were burned before the wildfire could be suppressed by state, federal and private crews that totaled nearly 600 men. With the poor level of radio contact available at the time, crews were in constant danger of being trapped by spot fires. Fighting both night and day to save the watershed, community members answered the call for flashlights, lanterns, canteens and hand tools. Timber operators responded with bulldozers, water tankers and line crews. Even the privately owned town swimming pool, Twin Plunges, offered firefighters a break, allowing them to take free showers, swimsuits and towels. It gave them the chance to swim a few laps before returning to the fight.

A lot was contributed to the final containment and saving of the fourteen-thousand-acre watershed and town. The winds did eventually die down, and an old fire break previously built by the Civilian Conservation Corps in the 1930s was successfully enlarged, coupled with backfiring. Three hundred thousand gallons of old mine shaft water was pumped from the Skyline Gold Mine, high above the burning fire, to mop-up crews via two miles of hose lines that had been donated by the Elk Lumber Company. Praise was universal for all of the various entities that helped fight the fire and the extensive cooperation and coordination between them. Fire crew mop-up continued for some time, while locals reclaimed the several hundred flashlights and tools that they had generously loaned to night crews. Seven more performances of *Antony and Cleopatra* were scheduled for the rest of the 1959 season, yet it seems unlikely that any matched the drama of the August 8 performance.

25

A Witness to History
in Our Midst

Not a passive viewer, Alfred Willstatter was an active participant in the twentieth century's most significant events.

Longtime Ashland residents probably know Al as the guy who owned and operated the town swimming pool, Twin Plunges, in the 1960s and 1970s. Or, perhaps, they remember him as the survivor of a nasty city council recall attempt in 1970. It is likely, however, that fewer know him as a survivor of the Holocaust or as an army interrogator for the Nuremberg War Crimes Trials.

Alfred Willstatter was born in 1925 to a Jewish family who lived nearby the gothic-looking prison where Adolph Hitler had been incarcerated a year earlier. It was there, in the picturesque town of Landsberg, that, while serving time for treason, Hitler composed his manifesto *Mein Kampf* and his plans for the Third Reich. Just eleven years later, with Hitler firmly in power, Al was forced to leave Landsberg, his parents and what had been an idyllic childhood.

Al remembered that the entertainment for young boys in Landsberg was simple and ample, with the Lech River providing their summer recreation and the steep hills providing winter skiing and sledding. There were the predictable snowball fights, homemade slingshots and toy tin soldiers to line up for battle, yet this all changed. While his friends were joining Hitler Youth groups that were being formed at his school, Al could not and didn't really understand why. At the age of eleven, he couldn't comprehend why

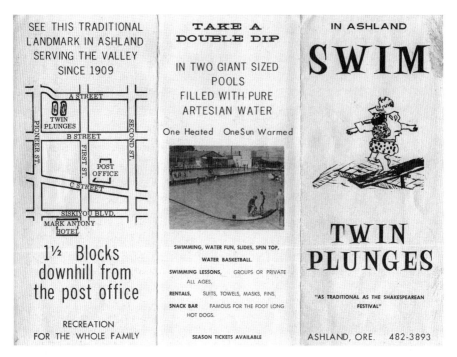

A 1960s Twin Plunges *advertising brochure. Courtesy of the Willstatter collection.*

being born into a family of Jewish faith was enough to deem him and his family enemies of their own country. After all, their neighbors always shared dinners with them during Christmas and Hanukah, exchanging favorite foods and wine. Passover was celebrated in their home each year, with Al's boyhood friends eagerly awaiting his mother's creations that came fresh from the oven. Just before he was expelled from public school in 1936, Al remembered, as a member of one of seven Jewish families in town, being marched from the school to the city square. He eventually realized that they were there to salute and listen to Germany's leader, Adolf Hitler. Al couldn't remember for sure, but he thought that he followed directions and shouted out "Heil Hitler," with his right arm raised, as he and his classmates had been instructed.

In the next two years, it became increasingly apparent to Al's parents that they must get their two sons out of Germany. In what had to have been the most difficult decision for his parents to make, Al and his brother Helmut were sent, in 1938, to distant relatives in America for their safety. Fortunately, his father's cousins, who lived in St. Paul, Minnesota, agreed to be sponsors for them. The United States, in the midst of an enormous

Al Willstatter and his brother, Helmut, with their parents in Germany prior to being sent to St. Paul, Minnesota, in 1938 to live with relatives. Al's parents were able to flee Germany in 1940. *Courtesy of the Willstatter collection.*

financial depression, only admitted refugees with relatives who were willing to show that they could provide financially for them. This made it very difficult to get an entire family out; often, only an oldest son was sent. For two years, Al's parents were protected by a group of Christian friends and neighbors. They had been provided with money, food and a means of getting to Genoa, Italy, until 1940, when they were able to escape on a ship bound for America and reunite with their sons. These efforts saved them from a concentration camp.

Being assigned to the first grade in St. Paul at the ages of twelve and thirteen was enough incentive for the Willstatter boys to learn English quickly and immerse themselves in American culture. Al admitted that the only English he knew when he arrived in the United States was "I am hungry" and "cheese sandwich." He played football and hockey in

Young Al and Helmut enjoying a happy childhood in Landsberg before the town was declared "free of Jews" in 1936. *Courtesy of the Willstatter collection.*

high school, and eventually acquired midwestern English language skills without a German accent. After graduating from high school in 1944, Willstatter enlisted in the U.S. Army. No longer an escapee from Germany, Willstatter crossed the Atlantic and returned to Europe as a thoroughly Americanized liberator. He saw combat action in the final days of the Battle of the Bulge and was involved in the liberation of the Mauthausen and Ohrdruf concentration camps.

Many young German men of Jewish faith who had escaped to America joined the U.S. military as a kind of vendetta, a duty, a crusade against Hitler and the Nazis who had driven them from their homeland. Al saw military service as a way to repay his adopted country for taking him in and saving him from death in a concentration camp. It was not retribution for the horrors that were brought about by the Nazis so much as a way to defend his new American way of life. To this day, however, Al has chosen not to visit any Holocaust museums. He can still remember witnessing the horrible smells of burning human flesh and the emaciated skeletons of the inmates.

He just can't risk the inevitable flashbacks that would occur. As an eyewitness to this genocide, he has little time for those who try to deny it happened.

Willstatter's German language skills led to a military intelligence assignment in war-torn Germany at the end of the hostilities. Chaos reigned as Nazi officials tried to pass themselves off as simple refugees and avoid capture for their involvement as concentration camp officials and guards. Once the major leaders of Nazi Germany were tried and convicted at Nuremberg, those in charge of the death camps were tried next and sentenced. Not as easily identified, SS (Schutzstaffel) guards and camp officials tried to blend in with the mass of refugees to escape prosecution. Screening them through interrogation was often the task of specially trained U.S. Army intelligence units, such as the one Al was assigned to.

In preparation for interrogation, Al's lessons involved a complete immersion in German military hierarchy and an understanding of the Germans' pride of organization and rank. SS units were especially prideful and went to some lengths to display their machoism. Many that Al interrogated had an "SS" tattoo in their armpit, which was their downfall. Trying to separate the concentration camp enforcers from those who were simply displaced war refugees became relatively easy, as a number of the SS displayed burns under their arms. Explanations of the burns usually included stories of them burning themselves while lighting a cigarette. Al had none of it and put them in the line headed for trial in Nuremberg.

After returning stateside in 1946, Al used the GI Bill to attend the University of Minnesota, where he met his future wife, Edie, in the German Department. Upon graduation, he was recalled to service for the Korean "police action" to work counterintelligence. After participating in refugee relief work through the U.S. Department of State in Salzburg, Austria, Al married Edie on Christmas Eve 1955. Returning to the States in 1956, Willstatter worked as a fraud investigator for the Los Angeles Department of Charities for several years. When he informed his friends that he was going to give up a secure and successful job and move to Ashland, Oregon, to buy and operate a swimming pool, they questioned his sanity, as did a number of folks in Ashland who had seen the pool sold numerous times.

Begun as a natural springs natatorium in 1909, the pool had changed radically by the time the Willstatters arrived in town. Once a massive building, the pool had been reduced over the years until it only included two uncovered pools, which were eventually sold for taxes. Its new ownership resulted in a name change (Twin Plunges), many upgrades and another reopening in 1931. Two more owners preceded Al and Edie, who assumed ownership of the pool in 1966. Despite the initial skepticism of some, the Willstatters ran a successful operation there for eleven years, before they sold Twin Plunges and the property was redeveloped. The location of the original pools is now hidden by the Ashland Food Coop store.

Forty-five years after Kristallnacht and the forced removal of Jewish families from Landsberg, a group of citizens formed an organization out of concern that this part of the town's history would be forgotten. Several years of effort led to a 2018 "Work of Remembering Conference," with three generations of Willstatters returning to Landsberg. Al's story, along with those of Landsberg's other Jewish families, has been highlighted and is now on prominent display in the town hall so that a much younger generation of Landsbergers can learn the fates of these families during the Nazi era. As Al has often pointed out, people are not all good or bad. Change is possible. He should know—he has been a true witness to history.

BIBLIOGRAPHY

Books

Atwood, Kay. Mill Creek Journal, *Ashland, Oregon, 1850–1860*. Ashland: Self-published, 1987.

Bowmer, Angus. *As I Remember Adam*. Ashland: Oregonian Shakespearean Festival Association, 1975.

Boyd, Brian. *Vladimir Nabokov: The American Years*. Princeton, NJ: Princeton University Press, 1991.

Clapp, John, and Edwin Edgett. *Players of the Present*. Reprint of 1901 edition, Lenox Hill, NY, 1970.

Enders, John. *Lithia Park: The Heart and Soul of Ashland*. Ashland, OR: D'Aimee Publishing, 2016.

Etulain, Richard W. *Lincoln and Oregon Country Politics in the Civil War Era*. Corvallis: Oregon State University Press, 2013.

Hall, Patricia. *Johnny Gruelle, Creator of Raggedy Ann and Andy*. Gretna, LA: Pelican Publishing Company, 1993.

Henderson, Bruce. *Sons and Soldiers*. New York: HarperCollins, 2017.

Keach, Stacy. *All in All*. Guilford, CT: Lyons Press, 2013.

Lewis, Gary. *John Nosler Going Ballistic*. Bend, OR: Gary Lewis Outdoors, 2005.

Martin, Robert Sidney, ed. *Carnegie Denied*. Westport, CT: Greenwood Press, 1993.

McDermott, Terry. *Off Speed*. New York: Vintage Books, 2017.

157

Peterson, Joe. *Images of America: Ashland*. Charleston, SC: Arcadia Publishing, 2009.

Sanderson, Mary Jane. *Healing Hands: The Story of Susie Jessel, as Told by Her Daughter*. N.p.: Self-published, 1965.

Who, Marquis. *Who Was Who in America*. Vol. 1. Chicago: MacMillan, 1989.

Manuscripts

Mater, Catherine M. "Parsons Pine Product: Trash to Cash." The Business of Sustainable Forestry case study, a project of the Sustainable Forest Working Group. Salem, OR, 1999.

Oyler, Verne William, Jr. "The Festival Story: A History of the Oregon Shakespearean Festival." PhD diss., Los Angeles, University of California–Los Angeles, 1971.

Willstatter, Al, and Betty LaDuke. *Al's Story*. Ashland, OR: Self-published, 2014, 2015, 2018.

Willstatter, Edith. *From Nat to Now: A History of the Twin Plunges*. Ashland Oregon: Willstatter Trust, self-published, 2011.

Interviews

Fletcher, Drew. Personal interview, March 14, 2020. Ashland, Oregon.

Newspapers

Ashland Daily Tidings
Ashland Tidings
Democratic Times
Medford Mail Tribune
Oregonian

Journals

Deacon, Kristine. "On the Road with Rutherford B. Hayes." *Oregon Historical Quarterly*, no. 2 (Summer 2011): 170–93.

LaLande, Jeff. "Beneath the Hooded Robe: Newspapermen, Local Politics, and the Ku Klux Klan in Jackson County, Oregon." *Pacific Northwest Quarterly,* no. 83 (April 1992): 42–52.

Mahar, Franklyn D. "The Millionaire and the Village: Jesse Winburn Comes to Ashland." *Oregon Historical Quarterly,* no. 4 (December 1963): 323–41.

Sweetland, Monroe. "The Underestimated Oregon Presidential Primary of 1960." *Oregon Historical Quarterly,* no. 3 (Fall 2000): 329–35.

Articles

Ellis, K.R. "They Call Her Miracle Woman." *True Magazine,* February 1943.

Fried, Stephen. "Saved by the Bell." *Smithsonian,* April 2017.

Mark, Steven. "Save the Auto Camps!" *Southern Oregon Heritage* 3, no. 4 (1998): 28–32.

Scripter, Charles Eldon. "The Lithia Park Story." *Southern Oregon History Series,* 1975.

Seemann, Charlie. "Rose Maddox, Sweetheart of Hillbilly Swing." *Table Rock Sentinel,* March/April 1993.

Table Rock Sentinel. "Portrait of a Murderer." January 1985.

Thomas, Harold A., and Howard G. Hopkins. "Twenty Years Ago—The Ashland Fire." *Timberlines,* September 1979.

Toy, Eckard V. "The Ku Klux Klan in Oregon." *Experiences in a Promised Land: Essays in Pacific Northwest History.* University of Washington Press, 1986.

Walden, Sue. "Growing Up in the Railroad District." *Table Rock Sentinel,* March 1988.

Official Records and Archives

An Inventory, Historic Documentation, and Assessment of Cultural Resources at Lithia Springs and Winburn Camp. Compiled by Nan Hannon and Clayton G. Lebow. Ashland, OR: City of Ashland, December 11, 1987.

Lithia Auto Stores Archives. Medford, OR: Lithia Auto Stores.

National Park Service. *National Register of Historic Places: Ashland Downtown Historic District.* Washington, D.C.: U.S. Department of the Interior, August 1999, section 7, 83.

About the Author

Joe Peterson is a retired educator who has lived in Ashland, Oregon, for twenty-three years. He has taught history, political science and education courses at Southern Oregon University, and he has managed the federal Teaching American History Grants for the Southern Oregon Education Service District. He has also presented lectures for the Southern Oregon Historical Society's Windows in Time series and has previously authored three books, including *Ashland* for Arcadia Publishing's Images of America series.